W9-CCD-402

BARRON'S BOOK NOTES

WILLIAM
SHAKESPEARE'S

The Merchant
of Venice

BARRON'S BOOK NOTES

WILLIAM SHAKESPEARE'S

The Merchant of Venice

BY

Joyce Milton

SERIES COORDINATOR

Murray Bromberg
Principal, Wang High School of Queens
Holliswood, New York

Past President
High School Principals Association of New York City

BARRON'S EDUCATIONAL SERIES, INC.

ACKNOWLEDGMENTS

Our thanks to Milton Katz and Julius Liebb for their advisory assistance on the *Book Notes* series.

Loreto Todd, Senior Lecturer in English, University of Leeds, England, prepared the chapter on Elizabethan English in this book.

All inquiries should be addressed to:
Barron's Educational Series, Inc.
250 Wireless Boulevard
Hauppauge, New York 11788

Library of Congress Catalog Card No. 85-3971

International Standard Book No. 0-8120-3526-7

Library of Congress Cataloging in Publication Data

Milton, Joyce.
  William Shakespeare's The merchant of Venice.

  (Barron's book notes)
  Bibliography: p.106
  Summary: A guide to reading "The Merchant of Venice" with a critical and appreciative mind. Includes background on the author's life and times, sample tests, term paper suggestions, and a reading list.
    1. Shakespeare, William, 1564–1616. Merchant of Venice.
  [1. Shakespeare, William, 1564–1616. Merchant of Venice. 2. English literature—History and criticism]
  I. Title. II. Series.
  PR2825.M54 1985   822.3'3   85-3971
  ISBN 0-8120-3526-7

CONTENTS

ADVISORY BOARD

We wish to thank the following educators who helped us focus our *Book Notes* series to meet student needs and critiqued our manuscripts to provide quality materials.

Sandra Dunn, English Teacher
Hempstead High School, Hempstead, New York

Lawrence J. Epstein, Associate Professor of English
Suffolk County Community College, Selden, New York

Leonard Gardner, Lecturer, English Department
State University of New York at Stony Brook

Beverly A. Haley, Member, Advisory Committee
National Council of Teachers of English Student
Guide Series, Fort Morgan, Colorado

Elaine C. Johnson, English Teacher
Tamalpais Union High School District
Mill Valley, California

Marvin J. LaHood, Professor of English
State University of New York College at Buffalo

Robert Lecker, Associate Professor of English
McGill University, Montréal, Québec, Canada

David E. Manly, Professor of Educational Studies
State University of New York College at Geneseo

Bruce Miller, Associate Professor of Education
State University of New York at Buffalo

Frank O'Hare, Professor of English and
Director of Writing
Ohio State University, Columbus, Ohio

Faith Z. Schullstrom, Member, Executive Committee
National Council of Teachers of English
Director of Curriculum and Instruction
Guilderland Central School District, New York

Mattie C. Williams, Director, Bureau of Language Arts
Chicago Public Schools, Chicago, Illinois

HOW TO USE THIS BOOK

You have to know how to approach literature in order to get the most out of it. This *Barron's Book Notes* volume follows a plan based on methods used by some of the best students to read a work of literature.

Begin with the guide's section on the author's life and times. As you read, try to form a clear picture of the author's personality, circumstances, and motives for writing the work. This background usually will make it easier for you to hear the author's tone of voice, and follow where the author is heading.

Then go over the rest of the introductory material—such sections as those on the plot, characters, setting, themes, and style of the work. Underline, or write down in your notebook, particular things to watch for, such as contrasts between characters and repeated literary devices. At this point, you may want to develop a system of symbols to use in marking your text as you read. (Of course, you should only mark up a book you own, not one that belongs to another person or a school.) Perhaps you will want to use a different letter for each character's name, a different number for each major theme of the book, a different color for each important symbol or literary device. Be prepared to mark up the pages of your book as you read. Put your marks in the margins so you can find them again easily.

Now comes the moment you've been waiting for—the time to start reading the work of literature. You may want to put aside your *Barron's Book Notes* volume until you've read the work all the way through. Or you may want to alternate, reading the *Book Notes* analysis of each section as soon as you have finished reading the corresponding part of the original. Before you move on, reread crucial passages you don't fully understand. (Don't take this guide's analysis for granted—make up your own mind as to what the work means.)

Once you've finished the whole work of literature, you may want to review it right away, so you can firm up your ideas about what it means. You may want to leaf through the book concentrating on passages you marked in reference to one character or one theme. This is also a good time to reread the *Book Notes* introductory material, which pulls together insights on specific topics.

When it comes time to prepare for a test or to write a paper, you'll already have formed ideas about the work. You'll be able to go back through it, refreshing your memory as to the author's exact words and perspective, so that you can support your opinions with evidence drawn straight from the work. Patterns will emerge, and ideas will fall into place; your essay question or term paper will almost write itself. Give yourself a dry run with one of the sample tests in the guide. These tests present both multiple-choice and essay questions. An accompanying section gives answers to the multiple-choice questions as well as suggestions for writing the essays. If you have to select a term paper topic, you may choose one from the list of suggestions in this book. This guide also provides you with a reading list, to help you when you start research for a term paper, and a selection of provocative comments by critics, to spark your thinking before you write.

THE AUTHOR AND HIS TIMES

The red-bearded man holds the knife high, poised to strike at his victim's heart. The spectators are paralyzed with fear.

Can anything prevent him from gaining his bloody revenge? The powerful Duke of Venice has already tried and failed. The only remaining hope lies in a beautiful heroine, who has no weapons to draw upon except a quick wit and a courageous spirit.

This suspenseful scene from *The Merchant of Venice* by William Shakespeare has been reenacted thousands of times since the play's first performance in the 1590s, and it never fails to keep audiences enthralled. Along with the tragedy of *Hamlet*, it is one of the more popular and frequently revived of Shakespeare's plays. It is also one of the most controversial. Some readers and playgoers find in the play an eloquent plea for tolerance; others feel uncomfortable with its reliance on what they regard as anti-Semitic stereotypes. The critics, meanwhile, cannot even agree on whether the mood of the play is happy or sad. Some describe it as a light, witty comedy with no social message whatsoever. Others have called it more tragic than comic in spirit. In spite of all this disagreement, *The Merchant of Venice* remains as compelling today as it was four centuries ago because it comments so eloquently on universal themes—the drive for revenge and the power of love. As the British essayist William Hazlitt wrote in 1817, "This is a play that in spite of the change in manners and prejudices, still holds undisputed possession of the stage."

Just about everyone agrees that *The Merchant of Venice*'s author was a genius, the most skillful and profound dramatist in English literary history. Yet very little is known about the personal life and character of this uniquely talented man.

Indeed, the documentary evidence concerning the life of William Shakespeare is so meager that for generations amateur detectives, and a few serious literary historians, have been tempted to theorize that the works of Shakespeare were really written by one of his more illustrious contemporaries. Christopher Marlowe, Sir Walter Raleigh, Sir Francis Bacon, and even Queen Elizabeth I have all been named at one time or another as the true authors of Shakespeare's plays. A recent theory, which appeared in a 1984 book called *The Mysterious William Shakespeare* by Charlton Ogburn, contends that a nobleman named Edward de Vere, the Earl of Oxford, wrote all of Shakespeare's works— but pretended not to have done so because authorship would have hurt his chances to shine at court!

Everyone loves a mystery, and so the speculation continues. The real reason for the belief that Shakespeare was a mere front for some other author is the snobbish prejudice that only a person of aristocratic breeding and wealth could have produced such great writing. The story of Shakespeare's life, sketchy as it may be, demonstrates that genius may appear anywhere, even in a country village and an undistinguished family tree.

Born in Stratford-upon-Avon in April of 1564,

William Shakespeare was the son of John Shakespeare, a glove-maker and storekeeper, and Mary Arden. (It has become traditional to celebrate Shakespeare's birthday on April 23, the same date as the anniversary of his death. Like so much in Shakespeare's biography, this, too, is speculative.) William was the third of eight children. The Shakespeares were not wealthy, at least not by the standards of the London aristocracy, but they weren't poor either.

If Shakespeare was like most sons of prosperous tradesmen, he attended a local grammar school where he would have studied the Latin classics. The plots of Shakespeare's plays, which borrow freely from other sources, suggest that he was well read in both ancient and modern literature. However, he never attended a university.

The only documented episode in Shakespeare's life which provides any raw material for gossip was his marriage in 1582. Shakespeare's bride, Anne Hathaway, was seven or eight years older than he, and records show that the marriage license was issued on November 28. The engagement was announced in church only once—not three Sundays in a row as was the usual custom. Some five months later, in May 1583, Anne Shakespeare gave birth to a daughter, who was named Susanna. Some scholars conclude from this that Shakespeare had gotten Anne pregnant and had to marry her. This position is challenged by other scholars who either claim that it was not unusual at the time for an engaged couple to sleep together or that the documentary records are simply unreliable.

Two years later, Anne Shakespeare gave birth to twins, a girl, Judith, and a boy, Hamnet. At some time during the 1580s—we're not sure exactly when—Shakespeare went off to London to make his fortune in the theater.

We do know that by 1592 William Shakespeare had earned a reputation in London as an actor and playwright. In 1597, when Shakespeare was only thirty-three years old and still had some of his greatest work ahead of him, Francis Meres, a preacher and scholar, was already praising the "mellifluous and honey-tongued Shakespeare" as the equal of the great Roman dramatists Seneca and Plautus.

The theater was a very popular form of entertainment in Elizabethan times, so named for Queen Elizabeth I, England's monarch. It was enjoyed by all classes of people from the most educated to the illiterate. Shakespeare's acting troupe sometimes performed before the royal court, and as he became a shareholder in the company it is likely that he earned a comfortable living. Nevertheless, many Elizabethans felt that the acting profession was not quite respectable. (For this reason, no actresses were allowed on the stage. All the female parts were played by young boys.)

The Shakespeare plays we know today were written over a period of some twenty years, beginning in 1592 or a little earlier and ending with the playwright's retirement about 1612. *The Merchant of Venice* belongs to the early part of Shakespeare's career. It was first performed in 1596, which places it after such early plays as *Richard III*, *Romeo and Juliet*, and *A Midsummer Night's Dream*, but before his foremost tragedies—*Hamlet*, *Othello*, *King Lear*, *Macbeth*—and such later dark comedies as *Twelfth Night* and *The Tempest*.

Shakespeare lived during one of the most prosperous and exciting periods in his nation's history. England was in the process of becoming a great naval power and a leader in international trade. Elizabeth I, who reigned for 45 years until her death in 1603, was a much-admired and extremely shrewd ruler. She survived many threats to her power, including plots aimed at overthrowing her in favor of her cousin Mary, Queen of Scots and an attempted invasion by the Spanish Armada in 1588.

There was a great deal of interest in history and in the lives of the great men and women of past generations. Playgoers took it for granted that they could draw inspiration and moral lessons from events of the past. Even the comedies, like *The Merchant of Venice*, were often based on stories and themes drawn from older literary works or from folklore. No one considered such borrowing to reflect a lack of originality.

The Merchant of Venice is exceptional among Shakespeare's plays because it may have been inspired, at least indirectly, by a contemporary scandal. In 1594 the Queen's personal physician Roderigo Lopez, a Portuguese Jew, was tried and executed for treason. The Lopez case inspired a wave of anti-Jewish feeling, and was probably responsible for the appearance of several dramas dealing with Jewish characters, including a revival of Christopher Marlowe's *The Jew of Malta*. If the Lopez affair did serve as Shakespeare's inspiration, only a few hints of this remain in the text of *The Merchant of Venice*. (One of these is that the hero of the play may be named for Don Antonio, the pretender to the Portuguese throne, who was associated with Dr. Lopez.) In Shakespeare's hands, the Jewish villain became a complex character whose drive for revenge many playgoers can understand

and even sympathize with. And the elements of treachery and suspense are balanced with light-hearted romance, creating a drama which many audiences find more satisfying than Shakespeare's farcical early comedies.

We do not know the exact date of *The Merchant of Venice*'s first performance. Most likely it was in 1596. It was revived during Shakespeare's lifetime, for a performance at court before King James I in 1605.

After his retirement in 1612, William Shakespeare moved back to his hometown of Stratford where he lived the quiet life of a country gentleman. He died in 1616, survived by his widow and two daughters. (Hamnet, the only son, died in childhood.) Although Shakespeare had a certain reputation as the author of the Sonnets and several narrative poems, no one had any reason to anticipate at the time that his plays would be the basis of lasting literary fame, much less become celebrated as masterpieces of English literature.

Shakespeare does not seem to have taken any interest at all in preserving his works for posterity. As was traditional at the time, the rights to Shakespeare's plays belonged to his theater company and were not considered his personal property. In fact, Elizabethans did not usually think of contemporary plays as being serious literature.

A few of Shakespeare's plays were published in his lifetime in cheap editions. These versions contained a good many errors. Sometimes stage directions or comments written in by the prompters got mixed up with Shakespeare's lines. Sometimes the actual speeches were based not on what Shakespeare wrote down, but on what an actor who had played the part happened to remember.

It was only after Shakespeare's death in 1623 that some members of his acting company set out to produce an accurate edition of Shakespeare's dramatic works. This edition, called the First Folio, still contained some errors. One play which we now attribute to Shakespeare—*Pericles*—was not even included. A real detective mystery for Shakespeare scholars has been the effort to separate the words Shakespeare actually wrote from the many mistakes and alterations that crept into the texts of the plays over the years. Even today, scholars continue to debate over which is the correct version of some lines in Shakespeare's plays. But we can count on the fact that the plays as we know them are quite close to what Shakespeare wrote. We can be even more sure there are no "new" Shakespeare plays waiting to be discovered—though this does not stop some people from dreaming about finding a dusty manuscript of a long-forgotten masterpiece.

As for Shakespeare the man, he will probably always be a mystery. We know who he was. But we can only guess what inspired him to write as he did, or how his plays were related to the events and concerns of his personal life.

THE PLAY

The Plot

Antonio, a rich Venetian merchant, has lent a good deal of money to his best friend Bassanio, a charming and carefree young man with a tendency to live beyond his means. Bassanio has fallen in love with a beautiful heiress, Portia of Belmont, and he has reason to believe that she loves him too. If only he could marry Portia, Bassanio tells Antonio, his money problems would be solved, and he would be able to pay back all the money he owes. But Bassanio needs still more money to travel to Belmont and court Portia in suitable style. Antonio is not particularly worried about being repaid, and he wants to help Bassanio for friendship's sake. Since all of his capital is invested in ships' cargoes, he has no cash on hand at the moment, and therefore suggests that Bassanio borrow the money. Antonio promises to put up the collateral for the loan.

Bassanio strikes a deal with Shylock, a rich Jewish moneylender, to borrow three thousand gold ducats for three months. Shylock proposes an unusual contract: He will charge no interest on the loan, but if the money is not repaid in time, Antonio will have to give Shylock a pound of his own flesh! Shylock pretends that he means this part of the bargain as a joke. In reality, since he has been the victim of Antonio's prejudice, he is nursing a deep and bitter grudge against the merchant. Antonio, a generous and optimistic man, does not understand the depths of Shylock's hatred and cannot imagine that his business would fail and that he would have to pay this bond. Besides, he will have more money than he needs within a few weeks. He agrees to the bizarre terms of the loan.

In the meantime, we see Portia of Belmont with her maid Nerissa, discussing the arrangements for her marriage that have been set up under her late father's will. Portia, we learn, will not be allowed to choose a husband for herself. Instead, her suitors will have to choose among three small chests, or caskets—one made of gold, one of silver, and one of lead. The first suitor to pick the chest with Portia's picture in it will win her hand in marriage and her entire fortune. The losers must promise to remain single for the rest of their lives, not to reveal to anyone their incorrect choice, and to leave immediately.

In Act II of the play, two suitors try their luck with this test. The first, the proud and exotic Prince of Morocco, picks the gold casket. Inside the casket, he finds a skull and a scroll which warns that "all that glisters is not gold." Obviously, he has made the wrong choice. A second suitor, the haughty Prince of Arragon (Arragon = arrogant?), chooses the silver casket. He has won nothing but a portrait of a grinning idiot.

Back in Venice, Bassanio is planning a dinner party to celebrate his upcoming departure for Belmont. During the course of the preparations, his friend Lorenzo manages to elope with his secret sweetheart, Shylock's daughter Jessica. Jessica runs away from her father's house on the same night that Bassanio leaves Venice, taking with her as much of her father's gold and jewelry as she can carry.

Upon arriving in Belmont, Bassanio learns of the test of the three caskets and willingly tries his luck.

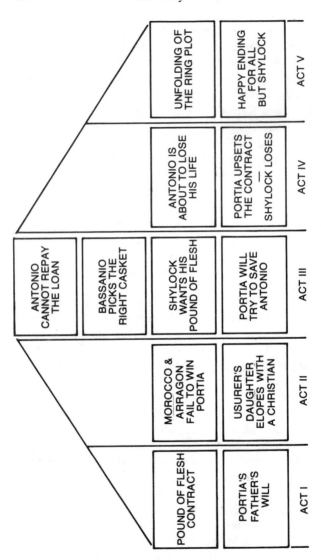

High Points in the Plot of
The Merchant of Venice

Reasoning that outward appearances are often deceiving, he chooses the lead casket, and so wins Portia's hand. Portia is delighted. She gives Bassanio a gold ring as a token of her love, making him promise never to give it away as long as their love lasts.

While Bassanio was courting Portia, his friend Gratiano has fallen in love with Portia's maid, Nerissa. This couple also decides to marry and Nerissa gives Gratiano a ring similar to the one Portia gave Bassanio.

The two pairs of lovers have little chance to enjoy their newfound happiness. Shortly after their betrothal, news arrives from Venice that all of Antonio's merchant ships have been lost at sea. Suddenly impoverished, Antonio is unable to repay on time the money Bassanio borrowed from Shylock. Shylock demands that Antonio fulfull the terms of the contract by giving up a pound of his own flesh. After a hasty double marriage ceremony, Bassanio and Gratiano hurry back to Venice to save their friend Antonio, leaving their brides behind in Belmont.

Lorenzo and Jessica, now married, show up in Belmont at the same time Antonio's bad news arrives from Venice. Portia asks the young couple to take care of her house while she and Nerissa go on a retreat to pray for their husbands' safe return. In reality, however, Portia has a secret plan. She and Nerissa arrive in Venice, disguised as a doctor of laws and his page boy, just in time for the trial which will decide whether or not Antonio must honor the terms of his agreement with Shylock.

At the trial, Shylock stubbornly insists that the law must award him his pound of Antonio's flesh. Bassanio, now wealthy, thanks to his marriage to

Portia, offers to repay three times what he originally borrowed, but Shylock has no interest in the money. He wants revenge for the way he had been abused—and if the loss of a pound of flesh costs Antonio his life, so much the better. Shylock is also angry over his daughter's elopement with a Christian. Portia, disguised as a young male lawyer, argues that while Shylock is entitled to his "bond" under the law, in the interest of true justice he ought to be willing to show mercy towards his enemy Antonio. Shylock rejects this plea.

Just at the moment when it seems Shylock has won his case and Antonio will have to die, Portia brings up another objection. Under the terms of the loan, Shylock is entitled to exactly one pound of flesh, but not a drop of blood. Moreover, Shylock could be found guilty of a capital crime for breaking a law that forbids conspiring to take the life of a citizen of Venice. The Duke of Venice, acting as judge at the trial, spares Shylock's life but orders him to convert to Christianity and give half his wealth to Antonio, who will manage it on behalf of Lorenzo and Jessica. In addition, Shylock must agree to leave his own money to Jessica and Lorenzo in his will.

Having saved Antonio, Portia decides to play a trick on her new husband Bassanio—who still does not recognize her in her disguise. Portia says that the only reward she will accept for rescuing Antonio from certain death is the gold ring that Bassanio is wearing. Bassanio hesitates, but when Antonio urges him to give it, he feels he cannot refuse. Later, Nerissa manages to get her ring back from Gratiano under the same pretense.

When Bassanio, Gratiano, and Antonio return to Belmont, Portia and Nerissa pretend to be very jealous. They accuse their husbands of giving away the gold rings to women—which, in fact, is true although Bassanio and Gratiano don't know it. Portia then produces the ring and hands it to Antonio. He, in turn, hands it to Bassanio who recognizes it as the same ring he gave the young lawyer in Venice. After more teasing, Portia finally admits that she and the male "doctor of laws" are one and the same person. Nerissa shows her ring and tells Gratiano that she was the lawyer's boy servant. Bassanio and Gratiano are delighted to learn that their new wives are as clever as they are beautiful. Portia, meanwhile, has one more piece of good news. A letter has arrived from Venice with word that Antonio's ships were not destroyed at sea after all. They have returned to port bearing rich cargoes, making him once again a wealthy man.

The Characters

Shylock

We do not know for sure how Shylock was portrayed in the earliest productions of *The Merchant of Venice*, but we have evidence that from the beginning he captured the imaginations of audiences. Although the play is named after Antonio, not Shylock, *The Merchant of Venice* soon came to be known by an alternate title, *The Jew of Venice*.

During the first half of the eighteenth century, Shylock was played as a straight comic villain—a whining fool. In 1741, a popular actor named Charles Macklin introduced a new way of playing the role. He made Shylock the epitome of evil, a malevolent old man consumed with hatred plot-

ting the downfall of his enemies. In 1814, the famous actor Edmund Kean presented an even more
startling version of the character. His Shylock was
dignified and austere, almost a tragic hero.

In some recent versions of the play, including a
movie adaptation, Shylock becomes so dominant
that we begin to see the other characters through
his eyes. A 1971 production of *The Merchant of Venice* created by the avant-garde director Peter Brook
ended with the sounds of Kaddish, the Jewish
prayer for the dead, being played as the ''good''
Christian characters gather in the final act.

Most scholars today agree that Shakespeare never
intended to make Shylock a hero. In all probabil-
ity, the playwright was not even very interested
in Shylock's Jewishness. He used the prevailing
anti-Semitic stereotypes as a handy way to char-
acterize his play's villain. What mattered to Shakespeare was that Shylock was an outsider—set apart
from society because of his religion, his profession
of lending money for interest, and his hatred for
Antonio and the other Christian characters of the
play.

Many of the most powerful works in nineteenth-
and twentieth-century literature deal with the pre-
dicament of an individual who, for one reason or
another, finds himself out of step with society. It
is important to realize that this was not necessarily
Shakespeare's point of view. The English of the
late sixteenth century believed that Christianity was
the only true religion and that the social order was
ordained by God. The individual who set himself
against the establishment could only be a source
of disruption or, at worst, evil.

Shylock's behavior during the trial scene (Act
IV, Scene I) shows us another reason why Shake-

speare cannot have intended him to be a true tragic
hero. A tragic hero would pursue his drive for revenge at all costs to himself. But Shylock, when
he learns that he might lose his own life if he sheds
a drop of Antonio's blood, immediately backs down.
Suddenly, he would be quite happy to have the
loan repaid in money and forget all about his call
for "justice." Many readers interpret that as the
behavior of a weak and unprincipled man, not a
hero.

Still, most readers agree that Shakespeare has
granted Shylock a dignity and depth of character
beyond what we expect of a comic villain. Shylock's motives may not be admirable, yet his character is realistic in a way that the characters of the
ever-cheerful, untroubled Bassanio and Portia are
not. It is impossible to listen to Shylock speak the
lines which begin "Hath not a Jew eyes?" without
recognizing something of ourselves in him. We feel
the sting of Shylock's passion for revenge, and the
sourness of his contempt for the Christians who
have tormented him. Shylock even speaks differ-
ently from the other characters in the play. He sel-
dom resorts to poetic imagery. His sentences are
short and choppy, emphasizing that he is cut off
from the others. At times, he almost spits out his
words.

The majority view of Shylock is that the contra-
dictory sides of his nature were written into the
part by the dramatist. Surely, in a play about the
virtue of mercy it is essential that the audience
should be able to see the villain's point of view
and accept him as a fellow human being, however
wrong or evil his actions might be.

In fact, the "debate" about Shylock is not so much
a debate about the character himself as about the

way the others in the play treat him. Whether Shylock receives mercy—or is the victim of a group of selfish, narrow-minded opponents—is a question you will ultimately have to answer for yourself.

Portia

Portia is in some ways a fairy-tale heroine. She lives in Belmont, a land of music, luxury, and perpetual happiness. Her father is dead, and we never hear about or meet any members of her own family. She is totally without problems of her own. All she lacks is a husband, and she doesn't even have to do anything about finding one. Under the terms of her father's will, the right suitor will be selected without any effort on her part. Everyone admires Portia, and from what we see of her their admiration is entirely justified. Portia is not only beautiful and fabulously rich, she is wise and witty, loyal and good.

At times during the play, Portia shows herself to be a very independent, even liberated, young woman. She complains about the terms of her father's will, and her comments on her various suitors leave no doubt that she is perfectly capable of choosing a husband for herself. When Antonio is in trouble, Portia conceives and carries out a rescue plan without even bothering to let her husband in on it. She passes herself off as a wise and learned lawyer with no trouble at all. We never seriously doubt that Portia will save Antonio. The suspense lies in seeing just how cleverly she will manage it.

It is easier to reconcile these two sides of Portia's character if you remember the Elizabethan view that true fulfillment and happiness can come only from accepting one's proper place in society. Nowadays, we tend to admire individualists. Shakespeare's contemporaries were more likely to regard them as troublemakers. Portia is independent, but she is not a rebel. Like Shylock, she is a strong character; unlike him, she is not an outsider. She uses her talent in the service of her husband and friends, and accepts her lot in life—that of the subordinate wife—graciously.

Even so, you may feel, as some readers do, that Portia stands out as more intelligent—even more powerful—than the male heroes of the play. Her most important scene comes when she enters the Venetian court dressed as a young male lawyer and presents an argument that frees Antonio from his grisly contract with Shylock. No doubt Shakespeare's fondness for plot twists involving young women dressing up as boys had a good deal to do with the fact that his heroines' parts were being played by boy actors in women's clothes. Audiences enjoyed seeing how a male actor would handle the double challenge of portraying a woman who disguises herself as a man. In this play, however, Shakespeare does not take the opportunity to milk the situation for its humor. Even when teasing Bassanio in the business about his missing ring, Portia is always in control of the joke. She herself is never made to seem ridiculous. She is as impressive as a man as she is as a woman.

Bassanio

Bassanio is an appealing character—ever optimistic, always impulsive. Even though he is already in debt, he is not particularly worried about having to ask Antonio for another loan. He thinks that he can win Portia's hand, and he does. Later, though he has promised Portia that he will never part with the ring she has given him, he hands it over to the lawyer "Balthazar." Of course, Balthazar is really Portia in disguise, and her demand for the ring is just a playful joke. She does not blame Bassanio for breaking his promise under the circumstances.

There are always a few readers and playgoers who feel that Bassanio is just a little bit too carefree to be likable. Some have even suggested that he is a fortune hunter. After all, the first thing he tells Antonio about Portia is that she is rich. Her other qualities take second place. Bassanio gets Antonio in trouble through his borrowing, and in the meantime rushes off in pursuit of a wealthy wife. Whether you agree with this view will depend on your feelings about borrowing, financial responsibility, and friendship.

Notice, however, that Bassanio never makes excuses for himself. In Act V, when Portia asks about the ring, Bassanio does not blame Antonio for talking him into giving it away. He takes the responsibility on himself. Bassanio's speeches also show him to be a young man of sensitivity and poetic feeling. Of all the suitors, he is the one who picks the lead casket because he understands that external appearances are unimportant compared to true inner worth. Perhaps Bassanio deserves even more credit for recognizing this, precisely because he himself has all the external advantages of good looks, social status, and charm.

Antonio

Antonio is the merchant of Venice, the character named in the title of the play. As such, Antonio must be considered the central character in the drama, yet in some ways he is also the most enigmatic. Antonio is rich, popular and confident. He seems to be a young man who has every reason to be happy. However, the very first lines in the play inform us that Antonio is in the grip of an unexplained depression.

You'll probably notice that the play presents two different views of Antonio's character. To his friends, Antonio is kind and generous. Although Bassanio already owes him money, Antonio does not hesitate to help his friend borrow more, even pledging his own flesh to guarantee the loan. When the loan cannot be repaid, and Antonio is in danger of losing his life to keep this bargain, he never complains or blames Bassanio for his troubles. In his dealings with Shylock, however, Antonio seems less than noble. When Shylock accuses Antonio of insulting him, even of spitting on him in the street, Antonio never denies these accusations. He even vows that he will do the same things again when the opportunity arises. You may feel that Antonio must be held at least partly responsible for Shylock's hatred of him. It is easy to be generous to one's friends. Isn't the way a person treats his enemies a good guide to his (or her) character?

Different theories have been suggested to explain it. One possibility is that Antonio is sad because his best friend is talking about marrying—foretelling the end of their carefree bachelor friendship. Othes feel that Shakespeare makes Antonio sad as a way of foreshadowing the bad luck which will befall him during the course of the play. Nowadays, we might call his gloominess a kind of "extrasensory perception"—ESP.

Another theory—rather extreme but accepted by some readers—is that Antonio feels an unconscious homosexual attraction to Bassanio and is depressed that his friend has fallen in love with a woman. You will have to decide for yourself whether there is any evidence in the play to support this interpretation.

Still another view of Antonio is that he is sad because he has chosen a way of life that sets him somewhat apart from his friends. Antonio condemns Shylock for being a moneylender, yet he himself is dedicated to pursuing profits in trade. While Bassanio, Lorenzo and Gratiano all marry during the course of the play, Antonio remains alone—too busy worrying about the fate of his merchant ships to fall in love.

Gratiano

Gratiano is a joker, the kind of young man who is constantly kidding around in an attempt to entertain his buddies. Bassanio takes him along to Belmont, but only after issuing a stern warning that he must keep his "wildness" under control. For the most part, Gratiano manages to do this. When he returns to Belmont for the trial scene (Act IV) we see a less attractive side of Gratiano's character. Of all those present, he is the only one who gets involved in exchanging insults with Shylock—and in gloating openly over Shylock's defeat. Gratiano's happy marriage to Nerissa seems to signal his acceptance into the fairy-tale world of Belmont. However, Gratiano never quite settles down, as we see from his continued fondness for bawdy jokes and puns.

Solanio and Salerio

Solanio and Salerio (in some editions of the play called Salarino or Salerino) are not popular roles with many Shakespearean actors. These young men have so little individuality that you'll probably find it almost impossible to tell them apart. They seem to have been written into the play mostly to comment on the plot and to keep the action moving along.

Since these two actors function largely as commentators, stage directors have a good deal of leeway in deciding how their role should be interpreted. In some productions, Solanio and Salerio reveal the darker side of Venetian life, expressing Antonio's unspoken prejudices by physically jostling and abusing Shylock. In other versions of the play, their roles are more genial and philosophical.

Jessica

Like Shylock, his daughter Jessica is a "problem" character for some theatergoers and readers of the play. When she elopes with Lorenzo, Jessica steals money and jewels from her father's house and then spends the treasure on trifles, including a pet monkey. Shakespearean audiences probably felt that Jessica was morally entitled to some of Shylock's money, in lieu of the dowry he would refuse her if she married a Christian. And her instant and complete adoption of her husband's point of view would have been considered proper behavior in an Elizabethan wife. Nevertheless, by modern standards, Jessica's lack of loyalty to her father, her people and her religion is unsettling to some readers and audiences.

Some readers see a change for the better in Jessica's character by the end of the play; having left her father's house and had her fling at rebellion (while spending his money), she settles down to the life of a mature married woman.

Launcelot Gobbo

At the start of the play, Launcelot is Shylock's servant, the "merry devil" whose malapropisms (unintentional and humorous misuse of words) keep Jessica entertained. Just before Jessica leaves her father's house, Launcelot also departs to join the service of Bassanio.

Notice that at the time that he switches employers, Launcelot is warned that he will no longer be able to get away with lazing around all day and doing nothing as he presumably did when he worked in Shylock's house. It may surprise you to hear that Shylock, the hard-driving miser, tolerated such behavior.

In later scenes, in his new role as Bassanio's servant, Launcelot appears to have changed from a stupid country bumpkin into a more polished entertainer, whose puns are consciously designed to amuse his master.

Partly because of his inconsistency, it is generally agreed that Launcelot is not the most successful of Shakespeare's humorous characters.

Nerissa
Nerissa is Portia's lady in waiting and confidante. She falls in love with and marries Gratiano. During the trial scene, she is disguised as Portia's clerk.

Lorenzo
A friend of Antonio and Bassanio, Lorenzo elopes with Shylock's daughter Jessica.

The Prince of Morocco
Portia's first suitor, the Prince of Morocco chooses the gold casket and loses his chance to win her hand in marriage.

The Prince of Arragon
Portia's second suitor, the Prince of Arragon is cold and arrogant. He chooses the silver casket, and

thus also comes out a loser in the contest for Portia's hand.

Other Elements
SETTING

The physical action of *The Merchant of Venice* is divided between two settings: Venice and Belmont. The first of these locales is real, the second imaginary—a split that emphasizes the tension in the play between real-life problems and fairy-tale solutions.

The Italian city-state of Venice exercised a powerful hold on the imaginations of Englishmen in Shakespeare's time. In many ways, Venice was what England aspired to become. It was a major commercial hub and a center of international trade. Although geographically small, the city-state had a tradition of independence and orderly government the English admired. The cosmopolitan character of Venice was especially alluring. In the English imagination, at least, the well-traveled citizens of Venice were witty and sophisticated, enjoying as a matter of course such oriental luxuries as fine silks, sugar and exotic spices which were still relatively expensive in England.

On the negative side, there was a feeling that Venice's internationalism, and its devotion to making money through trade, represented trends threatening the traditional character of English society. For example, Venice—unlike England—had a substantial population of Jews and other alien elements. It is noteworthy that in *The Merchant of Venice* Shakespeare makes use of the traditional image of the Jew as an alien, plotting against the welfare of citizens.

Belmont, the second locale of the play, is an imaginary world of music, laughter, and domestic bliss. The scenes of the play set in Venice take place in public spaces, in the streets, and in the courtroom. The action in Belmont is relegated to Portia's house and garden. Venice is governed by a set of laws that bind even the Duke; Belmont is ruled by the fairy-tale illogic of Portia's father's will. Portia's father, of course, is dead before the play begins. Even the generation gap is absent from the idealized world of Belmont, as are the social restrictions that would have prevented a sixteenth-century heiress from acting as independently as Portia.

Some readers feel that Shakespeare intended Venice and Belmont to represent opposite sets of values. Another view is that the two worlds are complementary; Venice stands for the public side of life where business, law, and manly friendship predominate—Belmont represents the private treasures of the heart, including romantic love and an appreciation of the merciful side of God's nature. You might be able to think of still another way to express the contrast between these two places.

FORM AND STRUCTURE

If you associate the word "comedy" with movies or TV shows filled with slapstick humor and snappy one-liners, then you may be surprised to learn that *The Merchant of Venice* is considered a comedy. In dramatic terms, however, a comedy can be a play that makes a light, basically optimistic comment on romantic relationships.

As it happens, *The Merchant of Venice* touches on

some serious social issues, particularly the problem of anti-Semitism. Because of this, some readers are tempted to forget that the form of the play is a romantic comedy. There have even been a few readers, the same ones who see Shylock as a tragic hero, who have tried to argue that the play is not a true comedy at all, but a tragedy disguised as comedy.

If you look at the plot devices used in *The Merchant of Venice*, however, you will find that they are quite typical of romantic comedies, particularly the romantic comedies of Shakespeare's time. For example, the lovers in the play are kept apart by external forces, not by shortcomings in their own characters or incompatibility. As in other Shakespearean comedies, these forces include arbitrary laws and restrictions (the conditions of Portia's father's will) and cases of mistaken identity, often involving the wearing of disguises.

Another common feature of comedies is that the original problem is often less important and complex than the eventual solution. This is certainly true in *The Merchant of Venice*. At the beginning of the play, Bassanio's "problem" is supposedly that he wants to repay the debt he owes Antonio— even though Antonio does not care very much about getting his money back. Bassanio's "solution" to this problem, courting and marrying a beautiful heiress, promises to be pleasant enough for him but requires turning Antonio into a debtor himself and even endangering his very life. Only in the world of comedy would the logic of this sequence of events be accepted without question.

The Five-Act Structure. The following diagram may help you to visualize how the action of the play is structured around the "problem" of Bassanio's debt:

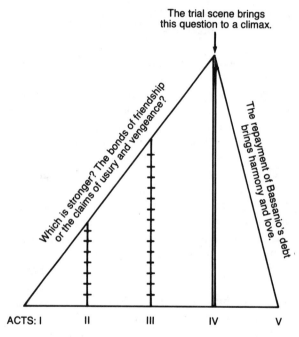

The trial scene brings this question to a climax.

Which is stronger? The bonds of friendship or the claims of usury and vengeance?

The repayment of Bassanio's debt brings harmony and love.

ACTS: I   II   III   IV   V

Act I: Exposition. Bassanio declares his intention to repay Antonio. The audience learns of the difficulties that stand in his path—the terms of Portia's father's will and Shylock's determination to revenge himself on Antonio.

Act II: Rising Action. Complications ensue. Other suitors arrive to compete for Portia's hand; the elopement of Shylock's daughter strengthens his desire for vengeance.

Act III: Rising Action. Bassanio wins Portia, but the problem of the debt is more urgent than ever.

Act IV: Climax. Portia's unexpected appearance at the trial enables Bassanio to repay his debt of friendship.

Act V: Conclusion. The "interest" on the debt is tallied up in the form of Antonio's restored wealth and the lovers' happiness.

Another view of the structure of *The Merchant of Venice* is that the action is circular: Antonio helps Bassanio to borrow money . . . which Bassanio uses to win Portia . . . which causes Portia to go to Venice to save Antonio. In this interpretation, the circle is completed at the end of Act IV of the play. Act V also serves to reemphasize the theme of circularity through the episode of the rings.

Another way of looking at the structure of the play might be to see it as a two-stranded braid. Woven together are events in two settings, Belmont and Venice, as well as threads of two different stories—the tale of the three caskets and that of the pound of flesh. Here, too, the knot between the two strands is tied in Act IV, when Portia comes to Venice and resolves Antonio's dilemma. Act V might be compared to the decorative tassel at the end of the braid—finishing off the play neatly and happily.

You can visualize the structure of the play by paying attention to the locales of the succeeding scenes:

	BELMONT	**VENICE**
Act I:		Scene I
	Scene II	
		Scene III
Act II:	Scene I	
		Scenes II through VI

	BELMONT	VENICE
	Scene VII	
		Scene VIII
	Scene IX	
Act III:		Scene I
	Scene II	
		Scene III
	Scenes IV & V	
Act IV:	Scenes I & II are both in Venice, but with Portia and Nerissa present there.
Act V:	The single scene of Act V takes place in Belmont, but with Antonio present.

HISTORICAL AND SOCIAL BACKGROUND

Two major issues raised by *The Merchant of Venice* are anti-Semitism and usury (which meant, in Shakespeare's time, loaning money at any rate of interest, not just at an excessive rate—as we define usury today). The following background information will help you understand these issues.

Anti-Semitism

The Merchant of Venice is one of several Shakespearean plays that create problems for modern readers because they are based on assumptions that we may find unpleasant and even repugnant. Many theatergoers today, especially women, have trouble enjoying performances of *The Taming of the Shrew* because the happy ending of this comedy is based on the heroine's acceptance of the principle that a good wife ought to submit to the authority of her husband. Some audiences and readers dislike the history play *Henry V* because of the manner in which it glorifies war and conquest. In the case of *The Merchant of Venice*, the troublesome issue is the anti-

Semitic portrayal of the character of Shylock. There is no way to ignore the fact that Shylock's character reflects some very nasty stereotypes about Jews. Not only is Shylock portrayed as being money mad, to the point of having lost touch with his natural feelings for his only daughter, but the motivation of his actions also draws on the belief, common in Shakespeare's time, that Jews were constantly plotting in the most bloodthirsty ways against Christians.

Of course, if *The Merchant of Venice* were merely an anti-Semitic propaganda play there would be no reason to continue to read and study it today. The play's continued popularity depends not just on other factors—such as the beauty of the language and the treatment of such timeless themes as love, mercy, and justice—but on the very way in which Shakespeare managed to rise above the anti-Semitism of his times to make Shylock a fully developed, even sympathetic character. One way in which modern readers come to terms with the anti-Semitic assumptions in *The Merchant of Venice* is to stress these counterbalancing factors. A few readers go so far as to deny that Shylock is the villain of the play at all.

Another way to come to terms with the value system of the play is to try to understand it in the social context of Shakespeare's times. In sixteenth-century Europe Jews were a despised and persecuted minority. England, in fact, went beyond mere persecution and harassment by banning Jews from the country altogether. In theory at least, there were no Jews at all in England in Shakespeare's time, and there hadn't been since the year 1290 when they were officially expelled by King Edward I.

For some time it was thought that Shakespeare had never actually met a Jew and must have created the character of Shylock entirely from his imagination. We now know that this was not necessarily the case. Despite what the law said, there was a small community of Spanish Jews living in London during Shakespeare's time. These exiles from Spain managed to evade the intent of the law by nominally converting to Christianity. Shakespeare may have been aware of this community, and possibly even have known some of its members. However, there is no reason to believe that either he or his audience viewed the existence of Jews in London as a major social problem.

One theory about Shakespeare's motivation for writing *The Merchant of Venice* is that he intended to capitalize on anti-Semitic public opinion aroused by the well-publicized trial in 1594 of Roderigo Lopez. Lopez, a Portuguese Jew who had converted to Christianity, had been the personal physician of the very popular queen, Elizabeth I. He was convicted and executed for supposedly plotting to murder his royal patient. We cannot be sure that Shakespeare had the Roderigo Lopez case in mind. Most likely, he did. However, a few historians doubt that this was so. They point out that during Shakespeare's time the English people viewed the Portuguese and the Spanish, their national enemies and rivals in trade, with great distrust. The popular hatred of Roderigo Lopez may have had more to do with his being Portuguese than with his being Jewish.

In any event, the most influential models for the character of Shylock were no doubt drawn from literature, not real life. The Jewish villain was a stock character in medieval literature. Medieval passion plays, reenactments of the story of the crucifixion of Jesus, invariably portrayed the disloyal disciple Judas Iscariot as a stereotypical Jew.

(Of course, historically, Jesus and all of his disciples were Jewish, but this was ignored.) The part of Judas was usually played for comedy, by an actor wearing an outrageous red wig and a false nose. Subsequent authors, when they portrayed Jewish characters at all, always cast them as villains.

A more immediate model for the character of Shylock in *The Merchant of Venice* was probably the character of Barabas in the play *The Jew of Malta* by Christopher Marlowe. In Marlowe's play, which was first performed in 1591, Barabas is a very wealthy Jewish merchant who lives on the Mediterranean island of Malta. Like Shylock, Barabas has an only daughter who is in love with a Christian. Barabas also has a rational motive for hating Christian society. In the play, he is angered by the passage of a law requiring all Jews to either convert to Christianity or give up one half of their wealth. Nevertheless, Barabas is a thoroughly evil character. He resorts to murder and treason to gain his revenge and enjoys watching the pain and suffering he has caused.

When we compare *The Merchant of Venice* to a play such as *The Jew of Malta* we can see just how far Shakespeare rose above the prejudices of his times. Shylock may be a comic villain, a stereotypical figure to some extent, but the play also insists that the audience accept him as a human being. It is no accident that many readers today find Shylock the most fully realized, even the most sympathetic character in the play.

Usury

The contemporary issue that Shakespeare had in mind when he set out to write *The Merchant of Ven-*

ice was not so much anti-Semitism as usury. To-day, the word usury means lending money at excessively high rates of interest. In Shakespeare's time, any loan made for interest was usury, regardless of the rate charged. Nowadays, usury in this sense of the word is not a social issue, except in a very few countries. It may be true that no one enjoys owing money, but the average American, for instance, takes payment of interest completely for granted.

During the Middle Ages, however, most European countries had laws against usury. These laws were based on the Christian church's view that usury was forbidden by the Bible. Churchmen called attention to a passage in Deuteronomy: "Thou shalt not lend upon usury to thy brother; usury of money, usury of victuals, usury of any thing that is lent upon usury: Unto a stranger thou mayest lend upon usury." Since in the New Testament Jesus had chased moneylenders out of the temple, most Christian theologians felt that the prohibition against usury carried over to Christians as well. All Christians were brothers in theory; therefore they could not charge each other interest. Jews, however, according to Deuteronomy, could charge interest to Christians, though not to other Jews. Laws which kept Jewish minorities from entering into many occupations encouraged Jews in many countries to take advantage of this interpretation of the law and go into the business of moneylending.

By Shakespeare's time, changing economic conditions had made the Church's traditional position on usury impractical to say the least. In medieval times, the typical individual borrowed money only in cases of dire need. By the sixteenth century, however, the economy had developed to a point where businessmen needed to borrow money in the everyday course of conducting their affairs. It was no longer reasonable to expect that anyone would advance them money purely for friendship's sake.

Usury became legal in England in 1551, four decades before *The Merchant of Venice* was written. However, it was still a controversial social issue, and not just among the poor. By the sixteenth century, however, anyone who wanted to live well needed a constant flow of cash. There were more luxury goods available than ever before, but their prices were constantly rising. The young noblemen of *The Merchant of Venice*, cheerfully striving to live above their means, were all too familiar to Shakespeare's audiences.

In making the character of Antonio an international merchant, Shakespeare seems to recognize and accept certain social changes. Antonio professes to be against the practice of usury. Yet he himself makes a living by buying goods on a large scale and selling wherever he can make a profit. What is the difference between profiting from, say, a cargo of wheat and profiting from a loan of money?

However, the play does seem to be taking the traditional position of the Church that usury and brotherhood are mutually exclusive. It is Shylock's practice of lending money at interest, as much as his Jewishness, which sets him apart from the rest of society. Antonio and Bassanio seek out the moneylender Shylock of their own free will. They aren't driven to borrow by any desperate personal need, but by Bassanio's belief that he can use the borrowed money to make a good impression on Portia. At the end of the play, Bassanio escapes economic reality by marrying the heiress Portia and going to live in Belmont. However, Antonio is left in Venice where, we suppose, he will continue doing business as before. Shylock, of course, has been condemned for trying to turn usury into a weapon of revenge, for scheming to get his "pound of flesh." Yet at the same time he has been given a speech which reminds us forcefully that money-lenders, and Jews, are human beings like anyone else.

Ultimately, you will have to decide for yourself what *The Merchant of Venice* is trying to say about the social issues of Jews vs. Christians and mon-eylenders vs. debtors. Remember, just because a work of literature is a classic, there is no require-ment that you have to approve or agree with every message it contains. On the other hand, the more you learn about the play and its social context, the more you may come to discover and appreciate the complexities of its views of human nature and so-cial relationships.

THEMES

1. LOVE AND WEALTH

Many works of literature deal with conflicts be-tween love and money. In *The Merchant of Venice* Shakespeare takes a more unusual approach to this subject, treating love as just another form of wealth. Love and money are alike, Shakespeare seems to be saying, in that they are blessings to those who can pursue them in the right spirit. On the other hand, those who are too possessive, too greedy, will get pleasure neither from the pursuit of ro-mantic love nor from the accumulation of wealth. Bassanio sets out to win Portia's love, solving his money problems at the same time. Shylock, in contrast, is a miser who hoards both his gold and his love and loses his daughter and his riches simultaneously. Antonio demonstrates the love of one friend for another by pledging his own flesh to guarantee a loan for Bassanio. He, too, is rewarded for his generosity. Not only do Antonio's ships come in at the end of the play, but Bassanio's fortunate marriage enriches Antonio as well, bringing him Portia's loyalty and friendship.

2.   MERCY VERSUS REVENGE

A number of Shakespeare's plays are concerned with the question of justice and the nature of legitimate authority. *The Merchant of Venice* poses the question of whether the law should be tempered by mercy, or whether it should be morally neutral. If neutral, then the law can become a tool in the hands of men such as Shylock, who use it to further their own personal vendettas. In Act IV of the play, we find Portia arguing that the justice of the state, like God's justice, ought to be merciful. Mercy does triumph eventually in this courtroom scene, but not until Portia reveals a legal loophole which makes it possible for the Duke to rule in her favor. In the world of this comedy, at least, the conflict between morally neutral law and merciful law is easily resolved. Readers do disagree, however, as to how well the theme of mercy's triumph over revenge is carried out by the "good" characters' treatment of Shylock. You will have to decide for yourself whether Shylock's punishment at the end of the trial scene is truly merciful—or whether he in fact becomes the victim of an unconscious streak of vengefulness in the character of Antonio.

3. HARMONY

As you read the play, you may find sub-themes which contrast other sets of values, in addition to those of mercy and revenge. For example, the test of the three caskets points out the truth that external beauty and inner worth are not always found together. On the whole, however, the play stresses harmony, not conflict. The play seems to tell us that in a well-balanced life the pursuit and enjoyment of money, romantic love, and deep friendship will not necessarily conflict. It is possible to experience and enjoy all of these things—but only if we do not place undue importance on gaining any one of them.

The theme of harmony is stressed throughout the play by the use of music and musical imagery. Portia and Lorenzo both praise and enjoy music for its power to ease sorrowful moments and make us more reflective in times of happiness. Notice, too, that Shylock—the character who is out of harmony with his society—fears the power of music. He even orders his daughter to close up the house to keep out the music of the masque.

4. FRIENDSHIP

It is not only romantic love that is discussed as a form of wealth in *The Merchant of Venice*. Friendship, too, is an important aspect of "love's wealth." Today, you sometimes hear the idea expressed that a husband and wife ought to be each other's best friends; a happy marriage takes precedence over outside friendships. Shakespeare's audience would no doubt have found this notion rather bizarre—suitable, perhaps for starry-eyed and headstrong young lovers, but hardly the basis for life-long happiness. In the play, Portia

demonstrates her depth of character by understanding that her husband's happiness depends
on his ability to discharge his obligations as a
friend. Thus, his loyalties have become her loyalties. Much more than today, the Elizabethans expected friendship to be the glue that held together business relationships between social
equals. You will notice that Shylock's refusal to
dine with Bassanio is treated in the play as an act
of hostility. This was a common view in Elizabethan times; religious and dietary laws which kept
Jews from socializing with Christians on a friendly
basis were seen as sinister, an expression of untrustworthy intentions.

5.   APPEARANCES CAN BE DECEIVING

The Merchant of Venice warns us repeatedly that
outer beauty is not necessarily evidence of inner
worth. As the motto on the gold casket puts it:
"All that glisters is not gold." Some readers feel
that the emphasis on this moral is out of place in
the play. After all, Portia the heroine turns out to
be as good and wise as she is beautiful and rich.
Another way of looking at this theme's relation to
the action is to say that Shakespeare has gone beyond the obvious, cliched implications of his theme
to hit on a deeper reality. Even a beautiful, desir-
able woman deserves to be loved for her inner self,
not just collected like an object of art. The rewards
from all worthwhile relationships can be achieved
only when the partners open their hearts to each
other. By the same reasoning, money itself is not
necessarily a bad thing—but you must be careful
to love it for the good it can do. Shylock's failing
is not that he is rich, but that he seeks to use his
money for an evil end—revenge.

STYLE

Language is the greatest expression of Shakespeare's genius, a leading reason why his works are still read and enjoyed nearly four centuries after they were written. At the same time Shakespeare's language can be intimidating. When you pick up a Shakespearean play, the first thing you will notice is that the characters speak poetry, not prose. Your immediate reaction may be that this is artificial and stilted. No human being talks the way Shakespeare's characters do. If you feel that way, you are absolutely right. The poetry in Shakespeare's plays was not meant to be realistic. Spoken poetry is an artistic convention—just like singing in opera, or surreal editing in a rock video. Just as you can appreciate the succession of images in a video without caring about whether they are realistic, you can enjoy the beautiful phrases, apt images and surprising insights in Shakespeare without bothering to worry whether any real-life individual would think to say such things spontaneously.

It is impossible to explain in a few brief paragraphs exactly why Shakespeare's use of language is so special. However, a few examples may sharpen your appreciation of his unique style.

Any writer might observe that young aristocrats are like proud ships. Shakespeare would never have been content with such a flat, unilluminating comparison. In Act II, Scene VI, he has Gratiano say:

How like a younger or a prodigal
The scarfed bark puts from her native bay,
Hugged and embraced by the strumpet wind!
How like the prodigal doth she return,
With over-weathered ribs and ragged sails,
Lean, rent, and beggared by the strumpet wind!

Few writers can carry a simile even this far without falling prey to muddled thinking, yet this is only one of several passages in which Shakespeare makes extended comparisons between the young gentlemen of Venice and their merchant ships.

Fewer writers still can use stylized, self-consciously poetic imagery without sounding pompous. Shakespeare's images are not merely pretty; they are almost always logical and apt. Furthermore, Shakespeare had an unerring sense of timing, a necessary quality in a playwright. He knew when to change pace for dramatic effect. Consider, for example, Bassanio's speech in Act I, Scene I, lines 123–138. Bassanio uses many high-sounding words to describe his problem. When it comes down to the final line of his speech, though, he manages to shift gears and sum up the situation in words of one syllable—"How to get clear of all the debts I owe." The audience, having been carried along on Bassanio's lofty rhetoric, is suddenly let down to earth with a thud.

One of the particular strengths of *The Merchant of Venice* is that the language used by the various characters is appropriate to their roles in the drama. Shylock's speech is gruff and straightforward. The Prince of Morocco's is as dazzling as his personality. Salerio, Solanio, and Gratiano are clever: in some of their speeches Shakespeare seems to be giving a virtuoso performance. If he crosses the line between exuberance and vulgarity, it's only to reinforce their characterizations.

Portia's language is perhaps the most unexpected in the play and goes far to show why audiences have found her such a memorable character. Although she is the romantic heroine, Portia's speech tends to be witty and rigorously logical.

She often uses a vocabulary that belongs to the world of financial transactions—words which draw our attention to the play's comparison of love and wealth, of money lent for interest and the emotional investments of marriage and friendship. Speaking of the "lott'ry of my destiny" (Act II, scene i, line 15), Portia goes on to note that her late father "hedged" his bet somewhat by the terms of his eccentric will. Suddenly, we realize that Portia is not referring to herself as a player in the lottery of destiny, but as the prize, waiting to be won.

Like most Shakespearean plays, *The Merchant of Venice* boasts many quotable lines—phrases such as "love is blind"—which you have probably read and even used many times without ever realizing where they came from. As you become more familiar with Shakespeare's works you will come to realize that such phrases are never just quotable nuggets, epigrams which demonstrate the author's clever "way with words." Shakespeare is a great dramatic poet because he knew how to use his best lines in context, to deepen our understanding of his characters and themes and to further the action of the play.

ELIZABETHAN ENGLISH

All languages change. Differences in pronunciation and word choice are apparent even between parents and their children. If language differences can appear in one generation, it is only to be expected that the English used by Shakespeare four hundred years ago will diverge markedly from the English that is used today. The following information on Shakespeare's language will help a modern reader to a fuller understanding of *The Merchant of Venice*.

Mobility of Word Classes

Adjectives, nouns, and verbs were less rigidly confined to particular classes in Shakespeare's day. Adjectives were frequently used adverbially:

> You grow *exceeding* strange
>
> *(I, i, 67)*

nouns could be used as adjectives, as in:

> And other of such *vinegar* aspect
>
> *(I, i, 54)*

and:

> By the *fool* multitude
>
> *(II, ix, 26)*

Nouns could also occur as verbs. In Act I, Scene III, line 170, for example, *purse* is used to mean "put in my purse":

> And I will go and *purse* the ducats straight.

And verbs could be used as nouns. In Act II, Scene IX, line 90, *commends* is used where a modern speaker would use "commendations":

> From whom he bringeth sensible regreets,
> To wit, besides *commends* and courteous
>   breath . . .

Changes in Word Meaning

The meanings of words undergo changes, a process that can be illustrated by the fact that *shuttle* has extended its meaning from a "device used in weaving" to a "space vehicle." Many of the words in Shakespeare still exist today but their meanings have changed. The change may be small, as in the case of *faithless (II, iv, 37)* meaning "unbelieving," or more fundamental, so that *sentences (I, ii, 10)* meant "maxims or proverbs," *very (II, ii, 105)* meant "true," *naughty (III, ii, 18)* was equivalent to "wicked," and *excrement (III, ii, 87)* meant anything that grew out, including one's hair.

Vocabulary Loss

Words not only change their meanings, but are frequently discarded from the language. In the past, *leman* meant "sweetheart" and *sooth* meant "truth." The following words used in *The Merchant of Venice* are no longer common in English but their meanings can usually be gauged from the contexts in which they occur.

argosies *(I, i, 9)* merchant ships
alablaster *(I, i, 84)* alabaster
ope *(I, i, 94)* open
moe *(I, i, 108)* more
neat *(I, i, 112)* cow
strond *(I, i, 171)* strand
colt *(I, ii, 39)* foolish, young person
throstle *(I, ii, 59)* song thrush
stead *(I, iii, 6)* assist, supply
bethink *(I, iii, 29)* consider
usance *(I, iii, 42)* interest
eanlings *(I, iii, 76)* lambs
pilled *(I, iii, 81)* stripped
doit *(I, iii, 137)* small coin
o'erstare *(II, i, 27)* outstare
cater-cousins *(II, ii, 130)* close friends
ostent *(II, ii, 193)* appearance, show
beshrew *(II, vi, 52)* may evil befall
cerecloth *(II, vii, 51)* cloth used in embalming
insculped *(II, vii, 57)* engraved
martlet *(II, ix, 27)* martin or swallow (bird)

Iwis *(II, ix, 67)* certainly
post *(II, ix, 99)* messenger
peise *(III, ii, 22)* weigh, expand
eche *(III, ii, 23)* lengthen
crisped *(III, ii, 92)* curled
magnificoes *(III, ii, 280)* dignitaries
bootless *(III, iii, 20)* useless
egal *(III, iv, 13)* equal
enow *(III, v, 21)* enough
meetest *(IV, i, 115)* most ready
cureless *(IV, i, 142)* without cure, irreparable
cope *(IV, i, 412)* give in exchange
and *(V, i, 176)* if

Verbs

Shakespearean verb forms differ from modern usage in three main ways:

1. Questions and negatives could be formed without using *do/did*, as when Nerissa asks Portia:

How like you the young German?

(I, ii, 80)

where today we would say: "How do you like the young German?", or where Bassanio insists:

I like not fair terms, and a villain's mind

(I, iii, 175)

where modern usage demands: "I do not like fair terms and a villain's mind." Shakespeare had the option of using forms **a** and **b** whereas contemporary usage permits only the **a** form:

a	b
What is the fool saying?	What says that fool?
	(II, v, 43)
What did he say?	What said he?
You do not look well	You look not well
You did not look well	You looked not well

2. A number of past participles and past tense forms are used which would be ungrammatical today. Among these are:

spoke for "spoken": "We have not spoke us yet" (*II, iv, 5); undertook* for "undertaken":

> 'Tis vile unless it may be quaintly ordered,
> And better in my mind not undertook
> > (*II, iv, 6–7*)

writ for "wrote":

> And whiter than the paper it writ on
> Is the fair hand that writ
> > (*II, iv, 13–14*)

flidge for "fledged":

> And Shylock (for his own part) knew the bird
> > was flidge
> > > (*III, i, 27*);

and *confiscate* for "confiscated":

> thy lands and goods
> Are by the laws of Venice confiscate.
> > (*IV, i, 306–7*)

3. Archaic verb forms sometimes occur with *there, thou,* and *he/she/it*:

> . . . there be land-rats
> > (*I, iii, 20*);

> What Jessica! Thou shalt not gormandize
> As thou hast done with me.
> > (*II, v. 3–4*);

> He hath disgraced me . . .
> > (*III, i, 48*).

Pronouns

Shakespeare and his contemporaries had one extra pronoun, *thou*, which could be used in addressing a person who was one's equal or social inferior. *You* was obligatory if more than one person was addressed:

> Lorenzo and Salerio, welcome hither,
> If that the youth of my new interest here
> Have power to bid you welcome.
> (III, ii, 219–21)

but it could also be used to indicate respect. All the characters, for example, address the Duke of Venice as "you" in Act IV, Scene I:

> Your grace hath ta'en great pains.

Frequently, a person in power uses *thou* to a child or a subordinate but is addressed *you* in return. Antonio, for example, uses *thou* to Shylock but receives *you* in response in Act I, Scene III:

> *Antonio:* I am as like to call thee so again,
>   To spit on thee again, to spurn thee
>   too.
>   . . . .
> *Shylock:* Why look you how you storm!
>   I would be friends with you and have
>   your love

To switch from *you* to *thou* could indicate a loss of respect. This happens in Act IV, Scene I when Portia realizes that Shylock will not change his mind about the bond:

> I pray you let me look upon the bond.
> (IV, i, 221)

> For, as thou urgest justice, be assured
> Thou shalt have justice more than thou desir'st.
> (IV, i, 311–12)

One further pronominal usage warrants a comment. Animate and inanimate third person pronouns were sometimes interchangeable. *Who* is used for "which" in:

> The first, of gold, who this inscription bears
> *(II, vii, 4)*

and *his* occurs instead of "its" in:

> There's not the smallest orb which thou behold'st
> But in his motion like an angel sings.
> *(V, i, 60–61)*

Prepositions

Prepositions were less standardized in Elizabethan English than they are today and so we find several uses in *The Merchant of Venice* that would have to be modified in contemporary speech. These include: *by* for "about":

> How say you by the French lord
> *(I, ii, 52)*

by for "for" in:

> What many men desire,—that "many" may be meant
> By the fool multitude that choose by show
> *(II, ix, 25–26)*

on for "against" in:

> And be my vantage to exclaim on you
> *(III, ii, 174)*

in for "on" in:

> . . . In such a night as this
> *(V, i, 1)*

and *of* for "from" in:

> No woman had it, but a civil doctor,
> Which did refuse three thousand ducats of me.
> *(V, i, 210–11)*

Multiple Negation

Contemporary English requires only one negative per statement and regards such utterances as "I haven't none" as nonstandard. Shakespeare often uses two or more negatives for emphasis, as when Portia asks:

> . . . is it not hard Nerissa, that I cannot choose one,
> nor refuse none?
>
> (I, ii, 25–26)

or the Prince of Morocco insists "Nor will not" (II, i, 43) or Lorenzo claims:

> The man that hath no music in himself,
> Nor is not moved with concord of sweet sounds,
> Is fit for treasons.
>
> (V, i, 83–85)

SOURCES

Shakespeare borrowed both of the basic plot ideas for *The Merchant of Venice* from other sources.

The story of the Christian merchant who risks a pound of his own flesh to secure a loan from a Jewish moneylender comes from an Italian novella entitled *Il Pecorone* (The Dunce) by Giovanni Fiorentino. In this version of the tale there is also a beautiful lady of "Belmonte," but she has only one suitor, Giannetto, who tries three times to win her hand. (All Giannetto has to do to win the lady's hand in marriage is to possess her sexually; what he does not know on his first two visits to her is that the wine she serves at dinner is heavily laced with a sleeping potion!) In the meantime, Giannetto's godfather, Ansaldo, has borrowed heavily from a Jewish moneylender to finance Giannetto's adventures. As in *The Merchant of Venice*, the lady of "Belmonte" eventually disguises herself as a lawyer to save her husband's benefactor from having to pay his pound of flesh. Even the sub-plot of the ring appears in this source; however, the sub-plots involving the romances of Gratiano and Nerissa, and Lorenzo and Jessica do not occur.

The story of the three caskets appears in a Greek romance of A.D. 800 called *Barlaam and Josophat*, and there are probably still-earlier folklore versions. We also find the three-caskets theme in a fourteenth-century story collection called the *Gesta Romanorum* which first appeared in an English translation in 1577. In the *Gesta Romanorum* version of this tale, the mottoes inscribed on the caskets are rather similar to those used by Shakespeare; however, it is the would-be bride who is forced to choose among the three caskets in order to prove that she is worthy of marrying the son of the King of Rome.

Shakespeare may not even have been the first writer to combine these two plots in a single work. This may have been done previously in a play called *The Jew*. Since the manuscript of *The Jew* no longer exists, we have no way of knowing how much, if any, of the dramatic structure of *The Merchant of Venice* was borrowed from this earlier drama. Some scholars have argued that the interweaving of the two plots is so skillful that it could only have been accomplished by a master dramatist, and therefore must be original with Shakespeare. Others are more willing to concede that the basic plot structure of *The Merchant of Venice* may have been borrowed by Shakespeare from one of his predecessors.

Either way, it is the eloquent use of both plot ideas to illuminate the larger theme of love as a form of wealth which raises the play to the level of a masterpiece—surely a Shakespeare original.

THE GLOBE THEATRE

One of the most famous theaters of all time is the Globe Theatre. It was one of several Shakespeare worked in during his career and many of the greatest plays of English literature were performed there. Built in 1599 for £600 just across the River Thames from London, it burned down in 1613 when a spark from a cannon in a battle scene in Shakespeare's *Henry VIII* set fire to the thatched roof. The theater was quickly rebuilt and it survived until 1644. No one knows exactly what the Globe looked like but some scholarly detective work has given us a fairly good idea. The Folger Shakespeare Library in Washington, D.C., has a full-scale re-creation of the Globe.

When it was built, the Globe was the latest thing in theater design. It was a three-story octagon, with covered galleries surrounding an open yard some 50 feet across. Three sides of the octagon were devoted to the stage and backstage areas. The main stage was a raised platform that jutted into the center of the yard or pit. Behind the stage was the tiring house—the backstage area where the actors dressed and waited for their cues. It was flanked by two doors and contained an inner stage with a curtain used when the script called for a scene to be discovered. (Some scholars think the inner stage was actually a tent or pavillion that could be moved about the stage.) Above the inner stage was the upper stage, a curtained balcony that could serve as the battlements in *Hamlet* or for the balcony scene in *Romeo and Juliet*. Most of the action of the play took place on the main and upper stages.

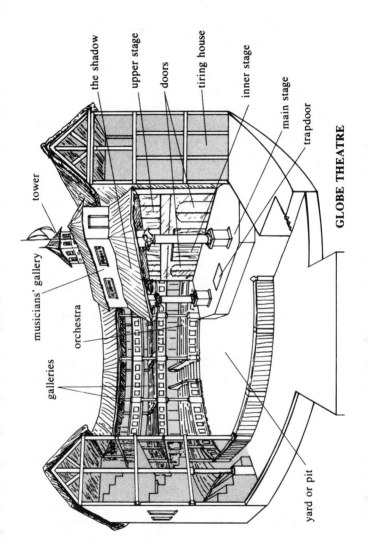

musicians' gallery

tower

the shadow

upper stage

doors

tiring house

inner stage

orchestra

galleries

main stage

trapdoor

yard or pit

GLOBE THEATRE

The third story held the musicians' gallery and machinery for sound effects and pyrotechnics. Above all was a turret from which a flag was flown to announce, "Performance today." A roof (the shadow) covered much of the stage and not only protected the players from sudden showers but also contained machinery needed for some special effects. More machinery was under the stage, where several trap doors permitted the sudden appearance in a play of ghosts and allowed actors to leap into rivers or graves, as the script required.

For a penny (a day's wages for an apprentice), you could stand with the "groundlings" in the yard to watch the play; another penny would buy you a seat in the upper galleries, and a third would get you a cushioned seat in the lower gallery—the best seats in the house. The audience would be a mixed crowd—sedate scholars, gallant courtiers, and respectable merchants and their families in the galleries; rowdy apprentices and young men looking for excitement in the yard; and pickpockets and prostitutes taking advantage of the crowds to ply their trades. And crowds there would be—the Globe could probably hold 2000 to 3000 people, and even an ordinary performance would attract a crowd of 1200.

The play you came to see would be performed in broad daylight during the warmer months. In colder weather, Shakespeare's troupe appeared indoors at Court or in one of London's private theaters. There was no scenery as we know it but there are indications that the Elizabethans used simple set pieces such as trees, bowers, or battle tents to indicate location. Any props needed were readied in the tiring house by the book keeper (we'd call him the stage manager) and carried on and off by actors. If time or location were important, the characters usually said something about it. Trumpet flourishes told the audience an important character was about to enter, rather like a modern spotlight, and a scene ended when all the characters left the stage. (Bodies of dead characters were carried off stage.) Little attention was paid to historical accuracy in plays such as *Julius Caesar* or *Macbeth* and actors wore contemporary clothing. One major difference from the modern theater was that all female parts were played by young boys; Elizabethan custom did not permit women to act.

If the scenery was minimal, the performance made up for it in costumes and spectacle. English actors were famous throughout Europe for their skill as dancers, and some performances ended with a dance (or jig). Blood, in the form of animal blood or red paint, was lavished about in the tragedies; ghosts made sudden appearances amid swirling fog; thunder was simulated by rolling a cannon ball along the wooden floor of the turret or by rattling a metal sheet. The costumes were gorgeous—and expensive! One "robe of estate" alone cost £19, a year's wages for a skilled workman of the time. But the costumes were a large part of the spectacle that the audience came to see, and they had to look impressive in broad daylight, with the audience right up close.

You've learned some of the conventions of the Globe Theatre, a theater much simpler than many of ours but nevertheless offering Shakespeare a wide range of possibilities for staging his plays. Now let's see how specific parts of *The Merchant of Venice* might have been presented at the Globe.

The absence of scenery made the stage at the

Globe very flexible. Scenes could be shifted from place to place without slowing down the action. You can get a good idea of how this might have worked out if you look at the second act of *The Merchant of Venice*. This act has nine different scenes. If a curtain had to be lowered and scenery moved for each scene it would take many hours to perform, and the audience would have been a little restless. But since there were no curtains or scenery, the action could speed right along. Imagine how it might have been performed:

The first scene, in Portia's house, could be set on the inner stage. For the second scene, on the street, the action moves out to the main stage. Then up to the balcony for Scene III in Shylock's house. Back to the main stage for the street setting of the next three scenes—one of the doors would represent Shylock's house in Scene VI, and Jessica would look out the window above it before she came down to elope with Lorenzo. Scene VII, back in Portia's house, could use the inner stage, then back onto the main stage for a street in Venice in Scene VIII, and finally a return to the inner stage, Portia's house, in Scene IX.

But don't assume that the main stage is limited to outdoor scenes. It would be needed as well for any indoor scene with more than a few characters. For example, in Act III, Scene II, the action might begin in the inner stage for the casket-choosing part of the scene, but would probably have to spill out onto the main stage to provide room for everyone when Lorenzo and Jessica arrive. Even so, once those characters have walked off, the neutral stage can become a street again for the next scene.

The Play
ACT I
ACT I, SCENE I

Lines 1–56

The Merchant of Venice begins on a street in Venice where Antonio, the title character, is walking with two friends, Solanio and Salerio. Antonio complains to his friends that he is feeling very sad but has no idea why. Solanio and Salerio try to be helpful by suggesting reasons for Antonio's glum mood: Perhaps, they suggest, he is worried about the fate of his "argosies" (merchant ships) out on the high seas.

If *he* were in Antonio's place, Salerio adds, he would be very worried about storms at sea. If you have ever had friends try to cheer you up, only to end up reminding you of all reasons you have to be *really* depressed—reasons you haven't even thought of on your own—you will be ready to appreciate the subtle humor of this scene. Instead of drawing Antonio out, his "helpful" friends force Antonio to defend himself.

Antonio denies that he is worried about his business. He has no need to, he says, since he never risks all of his money in one place. Solanio next suggests that Antonio must be in love. Antonio dismisses this possibility at once.

In that case, Solanio says, Antonio must just be sad by nature. Forgetting for a moment that he started out trying to lift Antonio's spirits, he comments unhelpfully that some people are just born with a "vinegar aspect"—a sour disposition.

NOTE: Antonio's very first sentence—"In sooth, I know not why I am so sad"—is one of many often-quoted lines in this play. In part, the line is remembered because it used to be taught to English students as an example of Shakespeare's main verse form—iambic pentameter. Each line in this form has ten syllables, with every two syllables equal to one foot (iamb). Every second syllable gets the strong accent:

In sooth', | I know' | not why' | I am' | so sad'. |

It is also memorable because it neatly sums up Antonio's mood. But *why is* Antonio sad? He dismisses all the obvious reasons his friends suggest.

Many different possibilities have been suggested to explain Antonio's sadness. A simple explanation is that Shakespeare is using Antonio's mood to set the scene. Although Antonio has no reason that he knows of for feeling depressed, his mood foreshadows the troubles that are about to begin. It tips off the audience that some development in the plot is going to interrupt Antonio's carefree existence.

Lines 56–190
Three more of Antonio's friends—Bassanio, Lorenzo and Gratiano—show up just as Salerio and Solanio are leaving. Gratiano also notices Antonio's melancholy mood. He advises Antonio to do as he does—"play the fool," talk and be merry.

After Lorenzo and Gratiano go on their way, Antonio and Bassanio become involved in more serious conversation. Bassanio admits that for some time he has been enjoying a standard of living puffed up beyond what he can afford. He already owes Antonio a good deal of money. Now he has a plan that would solve his financial problems and allow him to pay Antonio back. Of course, there is one small hitch. To put his plan into action he needs to borrow still more money.

Bassanio explains that he wants to court a beautiful heiress named Portia. He has reason to believe that Portia cares for him—she has been sending him "speechless messages" with her eyes. Nevertheless, there are many other wealthy suitors vying for Portia's favor. Bassanio needs money so that he can compete with his rivals.

NOTE: Bassanio compares Portia's lovely hair to the golden fleece, a treasure in Greek mythology. In the myth, the treasure was eventually won by Jason, the captain of a ship called the *Argo*. It is appropriate that Antonio's money, earned by merchant ships traveling the high seas, will be used to finance Bassanio's courtship.

Antonio readily agrees to Bassanio's plan. Unfortunately, he does not happen to have any cash on hand at the moment since all of his money is tied up in ships already at sea. He suggests, however, that Bassanio try to borrow money in his name.

You will notice in this scene that neither Antonio nor Bassanio appear to take money very seriously. It has even been suggested that Bassanio is a fortune hunter, taking a risky loan from a friend in order to make himself appear much wealthier than he actually is. But listen to Bassanio talk about Portia. He certainly sounds like a young man in love and not just a cold-hearted fortune hunter.

ACT I, SCENE II

The location of the action now shifts to Belmont and the home of Portia.

Portia's first words include "my little body is aweary of this great world," a complaint that echoes Antonio's in Scene I. Like Antonio, Portia seems to have more than her share of blessings. She is young, good looking and wealthy. And she, too, is chided for admitting that she is less than completely happy with her situation. In this case, the lecture is delivered by Portia's lady-in-waiting, Nerissa, who remarks that those who have too much good fortune often seem to be as unhappy as those who have too little.

Nerissa suggests that perhaps the secret of happiness is to be "seated in the mean," or to be average. "Surperfluity comes sooner by gray hairs," she adds, meaning that people who have more money than they need may end up worrying so much about it that they age prematurely.

NOTE: What do you think of Nerissa's suggestion? Is it really easier to be happy if you are average? And even if this happens to be true, is this kind of happiness worth settling for?

Considering what this play has to say in favor of the virtues of harmony and balance, Nerissa's philosophy may be taken to represent the point of view of the playwright. You might notice, however, that she and the other characters who speak in favor of the balanced, moderate approach to life happen to do rather well for themselves, both financially and romantically. Do you agree that too much money is likely to be a source of unhappiness? Or is this just a sentimental notion?

Unlike Antonio, Portia knows very well what is bothering her. She is unhappy about the terms of her father's will which prevent her from choosing the man she will marry. Instead, the will specifies that any man who wants to wed Portia must choose among three chests—caskets—one of gold, one of silver and one made of lead. The first suitor to pick the chest which has Portia's picture in it will win her hand.

This is just the kind of situation that you would expect to encounter in a fairy tale. In fact, Belmont is an imaginary place governed by fairy-tale rules. Shakespeare does not even bother to supply a logical reason why Portia's father might have set up this test for his daughter's suitor. Nerissa merely comments that since her father was a wise man he must have had some "good inspiration" for the arrangement.

Portia goes on to discuss her many suitors in terms that leave no doubt that she is a witty woman with very definite opinions of her own. As Nerissa reviews the names of the suitors, Portia reminds her of the faults of each one:

The prince from Naples cares about nothing but his horse. The Count Palatine is unbearably gloomy. The Frenchman, Monsieur Le Bon, is so shallow that he changes from minute to minute; "he is every man and no man." The Englishman, Falconbridge, has picked up his clothes and his customs from every country in Europe but can't speak any language but his own. The cowardly Scotsman is memorable only because of his hatred for his English rival. The German is a drunkard, and who, asks Portia, would want to be married to a sponge?

NOTE: Portia's witty characterizations of her suitors reflect certain prejudices about foreigners that were prevalent in Shakespeare's England. The playwright teases his audience, however, by including Portia's views on Falconbridge, one of their own countrymen. The English Lord has traveled widely and collected souvenirs indiscriminantly, yet he has never bothered to learn a foreign language.

Fortunately, none of the suitors Portia so dislikes has been willing to accept the terms of her father's will, which are that any suitor who picks the wrong chest must promise never to marry as long as he lives. He may not reveal which casket he chose, and he must leave immediately. Portia does recall one young man whom she liked, a certain Venetian, "a soldier and a scholar" named Bassanio. But of course, as she tells Nerissa, her own preferences make no difference. She is a prisoner of her father's will. As if to emphasize this, the scene ends with the announcement that still another suitor, the Prince of Morocco, has arrived.

ACT I, SCENE III

Back in Venice, Bassanio has approached the moneylender Shylock with a request for a loan of three thousand ducats for three months, to be secured on Antonio's credit.

Shylock agrees to make the loan, but he tells Bassanio that he will want to speak personally to Antonio. Bassanio then invites Shylock to his house, so that the three men can discuss the deal over dinner. Shylock, a Jew, refuses. He will not go to dine where he has to "smell pork." Doing business together is one thing, but, he tells Bassanio, "I will not eat with you, drink with you, nor pray with you."

NOTE: On one level, Shylock's refusal seems to be based on the simple fact that in dining with gentiles he might be forced to violate Jewish dietary laws. In the context of the play, however, the refusal seems to reflect a common Elizabethan view that anyone who refuses to share your food, as Shylock does, is hostile and untrustworthy. Later on, we will see Shylock set aside his scruples and go to Bassanio's after all, but for reasons that are not at all friendly.

At that moment, Antonio apears. In an aside—a speech heard by the audience but not by the other characters onstage—Shylock confesses his deep hatred for Antonio. "I hate him for he is a Christian," Shylock begins. Furthermore, Antonio lends money without charging interest, thus undercutting Shylock's business. Shylock calls Antonio an enemy of "our sacred nation" (the Jewish people) and mentions, as evidence of this, that Antonio has publicly denounced Shylock for practicing usury.

NOTE: The author of a novel can tell us directly what his characters are thinking. A dramatist does not have quite the same freedom. The audience must judge the characters in a play solely by their actions and their speech. The aside gives the playwright a chance to get around this limitation to some extent by allowing the character to "think out loud." Shylock's aside tells us a good deal about his motivations for wanting to make trouble for Antonio. But does it tell us enough? In a very few lines, Shylock gives a number of different reasons for his grudge. If you were in Shylock's shoes, which reason would trouble you the most? Why?

Speaking directly to Antonio and Bassanio, Shylock defends the charging of interest by citing the Biblical story of Jacob and Laban (Genesis 30: 31–43). In this story, Laban promises Jacob that as payment for his work in guarding Laban's sheep Jacob will be allowed to keep all the spotted lambs that are born. Jacob used cunning to increase the number of speckled lambs in the herd.

Shylock then reminds Antonio that in the past Antonio has spit on him and called him a "cutthroat dog." Does Antonio now expect Shylock to give him an interest-free loan, as between friends? Antonio assures Shylock that he has nothing of the kind in mind. He is ready to pay.

NOTE: Again, your opinion of Shylock will depend a good deal on which of his reasons for his hatred of Antonio you take most seriously. In his aside, it seems at first that Shylock was motivated by a hatred of all Christians. Next, Shylock added a more practical, even selfish, reason: Antonio has interfered with his ability to make a living. Now, when we hear that Antonio actually spat on Shylock in public, the balance of our sympathies might tilt in Shylock's favor.

At this point, Shylock suddenly becomes very friendly and assures Antonio that he doesn't intend to charge him interest at all. He wants to make friends, and so will lend the money out of kindness. Just for fun, he says, he wants to put a provision into the loan agreement that if Antonio fails to repay the money he will have to give Shylock a pound of his own flesh. Shylock innocently insists that he has no particular desire ever to collect this penalty. After all, he only cares about money. What profit is there in human flesh?

Bassanio, horrified, urges Antonio not to accept. However, Antonio insists that he has no worries about his ability to repay the loan. He agrees to the bargain.

Antonio even comments that Shylock "will turn Christian; he turns kind." This remark is apparently not meant to be ironic. Antonio, assuming that only Christians are capable of kindness, is naïve as well as unthinkingly intolerant.

Perhaps you know some individuals from your own experience who, like Antonio, are simply not given to searching for hidden motives, either other people's or their own. If we are to believe Salerio and Solanio, Antonio's naïvete on this score is evidence of his goodness; he is too virtuous himself to suspect that Shylock might be plotting against him. As you read on, however, notice what the play has to say about the conflict between external appearances and inner reality. Perhaps being too trusting is not a sign of innocence, but of shallowness. Perhaps Antonio is even a bit of a masochist—a man who unconsciously enjoys playing the martyr role. What do you think?

ACT II
ACT II, SCENE I

At Portia's home in Belmont, a fanfare of trumpets announces the arrival of her latest suitor, the Prince of Morocco. The Prince is an exotic, physically imposing man, tall and dark-skinned and dressed from head to toe in white. No one, however, could accuse the Prince of being humble. He immediately informs Portia that she mustn't hold his blackness against him—his blood is as red as that of any white-skinned northerner. And, he adds boastfully, women love his dark skin.

NOTE: The prince proudly calls his dark skin "the shadowed livery of the burnished sun," a beautiful phrase. Livery is a uniform, often very elaborate or showy, worn by the servants of the aristocracy. So the prince is saying that a dark complexion is the uniform of those who live close to the tropical sun.

Portia agrees that the Prince is as fair as any suitor she has yet seen, but under the terms of her father's will the Prince will have to take his chances like anyone else.

The Prince is not very happy with the nature of

the test that he will have to face but he's willing to take his chances. He has plenty of courage, he tells Portia. With his scimitar, he has killed a Persian king (sophy) and a prince, and done battle with the army of the great "Solyman," the Turkish sultan.

The scene ends with Portia inviting the Prince to have dinner with her before he tries his luck with the three chests.

ACT II, SCENE II

On a street in Venice, Launcelot Gobbo, Shylock's servant, is debating out loud with his conscience about whether he should leave Shylock or seek a new master. Launcelot is the clown of this play, a character whose appearance is the signal for an interlude of low comedy relief. Launcelot's reasons for wanting to leave Shylock at this particular moment are left vague. His speech is, for the most part, an excuse for broad comic acting.

NOTE: Launcelot describes his conscience as "hanging about the neck of my heart"—in other words, holding back his desires in the same way that a clinging woman might hold back her reluctant lover. On the stage, actors playing this scene typically use a high-pitched, falsetto voice for the lines "spoken" by Launcelot's conscience. The clown's conscience and his desires have created almost a split personality which struggles visibly for control of his body.

Launcelot's debate with himself is interrupted

by the appearance of Old Gobbo, his nearly blind father. Launcelot describes his father as "sand-blind," a twisted version of an old English word "samblind" which means half-blind. Old Gobbo is not only practically sightless, but he's as silly as his son. He does not recognize Launcelot's voice, and is totally confused by the nonsensical directions that Launcelot gives him for getting to Shylock's house. Launcelot even teases Old Gobbo by hinting that his son is dead. "It is a wise father who knows his own child," Launcelot says. In the context of Launcelot's speech it is just another absurd, throwaway line. You may recall it later, however, as we learn more about the relationship of Shylock and his only daughter Jessica.

No sooner has Old Gobbo finally recognized Launcelot, than Bassanio appears. Launcelot begs Bassanio to take him on as a servant.

Again, there would be no point in asking why Bassanio wants to have the muddleheaded Launcelot as a servant. Launcelot exists in the play purely for the sake of humor and as a direct link between Shylock and Bassanio.

At the close of this comic scene Gratiano appears and asks Bassanio to take him along to Belmont. Bassanio agrees, provided that Gratiano curb his "wild behaviour" and constant talking.

ACT II, SCENE III

Returning to Shylock's house to pick up his belongings, Launcelot says goodbye to Jessica, Shylock's only child. Jessica complains that "our house is hell" and adds that she will be sorry to see Launcelot go, for at least he has been a "merry devil." Jessica gives Launcelot a letter to be delivered to a certain Lorenzo, who will be a guest at the banquet Bassanio is planning to give that very evening. Apparently, Shylock's loan is already being spent to maintain Bassanio's gracious style of living.

After Launcelot leaves, Jessica remarks to herself that she is her father's daughter by blood, but not in manners. If her plans work out, she will soon be escaping Shylock's house to marry Lorenzo and become a Christian.

NOTE: The young couple in love who foil parental opposition by eloping together were a standard feature of Elizabethan drama. Audiences were prepared to take the lovers' side and did not normally waste much sympathy on the father who was deceived. In this case, there is the added complication that Jessica will reject her father's religion and convert to Christianity. Jessica mentions in passing that it's a "sin" for a daughter to be ashamed of her own father. However, she does not seem to be agonizing very deeply over her own disloyalty.

ACT II, SCENE IV

Bassanio is preparing a festive dinner party to celebrate his departure for Belmont. Discussing his plans with his friends—Gratiano, Salerio, Solanio and Lorenzo—Bassanio reveals that the entertainment will include a masque.

NOTE: The masque was a popular form of entertainment during the sixteenth and seventeenth centuries. The participants wore fancy dress and disguised their identity with masks. The evening included dancing, pantomime skits and, often, a parade through the streets. The best-known equivalent of a masque nowadays is probably the annual Mardi Gras celebration held in New Orleans.

Launcelot arrives with Jessica's message, informing Lorenzo that she is ready to elope. She's bringing with her all the gold that her father has in his house. Delighted with Jessica's plan to steal Shylock's gold and jewels when she leaves the house, Lorenzo adds that if Shylock ever gets into heaven it will be thanks to his "gentle" daughter.

If you are like most modern readers, you may find it hard to share Lorenzo's satisfaction over this development. It's one thing for him and Jessica to plan an elopement, quite another for them to cheerfully conspire to rob Jessica's own father! Audiences in Shakespeare's day probably had fewer qualms about the morality of this plan. Shylock, the Jew, was assumed to be in the wrong, and his daughter's desire to convert to Christianity was proof of her virtue. Notice, too, that these characters have absolutely no sympathy for Shylock's sober, frugal style of living. In an age when wealth and social position were expected to go hand in hand, to have money and not spend it freely was considered suspect, almost evil in itself. Wealthy aristocrats were expected to live in accordance with their status in society and to spread their money around. Businessmen, who became wealthy through hard work and thrift, were not necessarily admired. It is interesting to compare this outlook with the view that it is in bad taste for the rich to flaunt their position by "conspicuous consumption." Which philosophy of spending do you think is in style today?

ACT II, SCENE V

Bassanio had previously invited Shylock to dinner. Shylock suspects that he is not being invited out of friendship, but he decides to accept the invitation anyway. He will, he says, "go in hate to feed upon the prodigal Christian." In other words, Shylock plans to attend the dinner in order to savor the sight of Bassanio foolishly spending his borrowed money.

Before he leaves, Shylock warns his daughter to lock herself up in the house. He has dreamed about money bags, a bad omen. Also, he does not want Jessica to be exposed to the sight of the foolish revelry of the Christians' masque.

The very language Shylock uses emphasizes his materialism. He talks about his house almost as if it were a person. Ordering Jessica to shutter the windows, he tells her to "stop my house's ears" to keep out the sounds of the masque.

Launcelot, meanwhile, manages to pull Jessica aside long enough to deliver a cryptic message:

> There will come a Christian by
> Will be worth a Jewess' eye.

Jessica recognizes that this is a signal from Lorenzo. The elopement is on for that evening.

ACT II, SCENE VI

It is now evening and Gratiano and Salerio, dressed in their costumes for the masque, have slipped away from Bassanio's dinner party to meet

Lorenzo on the corner near Shylock's house. The two men comment rather cynically that most people get more enjoyment out of chasing happiness than they do from the happiness itself.

NOTE: This is one of several scenes in the play where the young Venetians compare themselves to merchant ships. Gratiano says that when a young man sets out from home he is like a ship departing from its home port, pennants flying. Later, after being hugged by the "strumpet wind" the same ship returns home looking worn and bedraggled, like a prodigal son.

Lorenzo arrives and leads his friends to Shylock's house where Jessica appears in an upstairs window, dressed as a page boy. Jessica, embarrassed by the way she looks in boys' clothes, consoles herself with the thought that:

> Love is blind, and lovers cannot see
> The pretty follies that they themselves commit.

You may wonder, at this point, whether Jessica's remark applies to more than just her clothes. Stealing money from Shylock is another "pretty folly"—at least in the terms of the play.

Jessica and Lorenzo escape, in the company of Salerio. Gratiano, meanwhile, runs into Antonio who brings the news that the masque has been canceled. The wind has changed to favor sailing, and Bassanio's ship is going to leave port very soon. Gratiano hurries to join his friend.

ACT II, SCENE VII

The setting is again Belmont, where the Prince of Morocco is about to try his luck at winning Portia's hand.

Portia pulls aside a curtain and shows the Prince the three chests, or caskets, among which he must choose. The first chest, made of gold, has an inscription which reads: "Who chooseth me shall gain what many men desire." The second chest is made of silver. Its inscription reads: "Who chooseth me shall get as much as he deserves." The third chest is made of lead. Its inscription warns: "Who chooseth me must give and hazard all he hath." Portia tells the Prince that if he chooses the right chest he will find her portrait inside.

The prince immediately dismisses the lead chest. His "golden mind" would not stoop to risking so much for mere lead. He is tempted by the silver chest, since in his own opinion he very much deserves the fair Portia. But it is the third casket, the gold one, that pleases him most. Obviously, he reasons, Portia is desired by the whole world. It would be an insult to her beauty to think that her portrait would be anywhere but in the most valuable and showy of the three caskets.

Receiving the key from Portia, the Prince opens the gold chest and finds . . . a skull! Inside the hollow eye socket of the skull is a scroll. The prince unfolds this paper and reads a verse which says, in part:

> "All that glisters is not gold—
> Often have you heard that told . . .
> Gilded tombs do worms infold."

NOTE: Most likely you foresaw that the Prince's choice would be the wrong one. In fairy tales, for some reason, the most obvious choice never turns out to be correct. Sigmund Freud, the father of psychoanalysis, wrote an interesting essay in which he compared this scene with various folk tales in which a suitor has to choose among three daughters. Invariably, the youngest and, seemingly, the least pretty of the daughters is the correct choice. Different writers have advanced many reasons why the homeliest daughter invariably turns out to be the right choice. Freud thought that the plain sister originally represented death. Storytellers over the years, in effect, reversed the meaning of the fable. By making the plain girl the choice that brought good luck, they were wishing death out of existence. A more obvious explanation is that such tales simply seek to warn us against superficial values. A flashy appearance is not necessarily evidence of inner worth.

ACT II, SCENE VIII

Salerio and Solanio, on a street in Venice, engage in a conversation that brings us up to date on Shylock's reaction to his daughter's elopement.

Salerio tells his friend that on learning of Jessica's elopement Shylock made a fool of himself by going through the streets wailing, "O my ducats! O my daughter!" The implication is that Shylock is a heartless man who thinks of his daughter as just another possession—like his horde of gold ducats.

Also, in the course of this conversation, Salerio

mentions hearing some ominous news. An Italian merchant ship has been reported sunk in the English Channel. He fervently hopes that the ship will not turn out to be one of Antonio's.

ACT II, SCENE IX

At Portia's house, another suitor has arrived to face the test of the three caskets. This suitor, the Prince of Arragon, is just as proud as the Prince of Morocco. Instead of being outgoing and boastful, however, he is cold and haughty. The Prince of Morocco at least admitted that when it came to a test of luck he would be on the same plane as any other man. The Prince of Arragon is sure that his intelligence and superior taste will lead him to the right choice. He passes over the lead casket without a second thought, remarking that he wouldn't stoop to risking all he had for mere lead. He also dismisses the gold casket. Anything that "many men desire," he reasons, must be for the common herd, not for him. Arragon concludes that the silver casket must be the right choice. He has no qualms at all about the inscription's promise that he will get what he deserves. This is a man who feels certain that he deserves to win.

Unlocking the chest Arragon finds . . . a picture of a grinning idiot! The Prince accepts this rebuke with remarkably good grace. Taking the idiot's picture with him, he says that he came to Belmont with one fool's head but will leave with two.

NOTE: Most readers have no trouble accepting that the gold chest, the choice dictated by greed, should be the wrong one. But why should the "wise" choice also be wrong? Doesn't this seem unfair? One possible explanation is that the Prince of Arragon's wisdom is not guided by love. The Prince of Morocco wanted Portia as a sort of accessory to his own dazzling image. Arragon wanted Portia because he thought he was *supposed* to want her. His very attitude towards losing suggests that he is not terribly disappointed at the thought of not being able to marry Portia—or, for that matter, any woman at all, according to his promise. One senses that love does not play a very large role in Arragon's scheme of values.

After the Prince departs, a messenger arrives with the news that yet another suitor has appeared—a young Venetian so courteous and so laden with rich gifts for Portia that he is a very promising "ambassador of love." Both Portia and Nerissa hope that the newcomer will turn out to be Bassanio.

ACT III
ACT III, SCENE I

While walking down a street in Venice, Solanio and Salerio discuss some recent bad news. The Venetian ship destroyed in the English Channel is Antonio's after all. The two friends wonder out loud how such a good, honest man as Antonio can have such bad luck.

Salerio and Solanio's good opinion does not extend to Shylock. Meeting the moneylender on the street, they immediately ask him what's new—knowing very well that Shylock must still be upset about his daughter's elopement. When Shylock mourns that his own "flesh and blood" has rebelled against him, the young men begin to taunt him. He and Jessica were no more alike, they say, than ebony and ivory, or red wine and white wine. What they really want to know, Salerio says, is whether Shylock has heard any more news about Antonio's ships.

Obviously, Shylock already knows about the loss of Antonio's ship. Antonio, he replies, had better not forget the bargain he made at the time of the loan.

Surely Shylock wouldn't take the pound of flesh even if Antonio did fail to pay his loan, Salerio says. What would it be good for? Why, for revenge! Shylock answers.

> Hath not a Jew eyes? Hath not a Jew hands, organs, dimensions, senses, passions. . . . If you prick us, do we not bleed? If you tickle us, do we not laugh? If you poison us, do we not die? And if you wrong us, shall we not revenge?

NOTE: Has it occurred to you that Salerio and Solanio—not to mention Antonio himself—were awfully naïve to believe that Shylock would not try to take Antonio's flesh? Although none of these men like or respect Shylock, it never occurs to them that he might hate them enough to want revenge for all the times he has been insulted.

Shylock's answer to Salerio's question is worth studying very carefully in its entirety. Some readers have called it the most powerful plea for tolerance in all of English literature. Others feel that it must be respected as the most forthright statement of human equality ever written, at least up until modern times. Certainly, it expresses in strong terms the conviction that all human beings share the same physical makeup, the same emotions and so, by extension, the same motives for good or evil.

Did Shakespeare intend this speech to be taken so seriously? Readers point out that Shylock never mentions the higher human functions, such as thought and spirituality. Animals also share many of the qualities that Shylock enumerates. They, too, can be made to bleed, they respond to being tickled, they die if fed poison. The last response that Shylock mentions is, however, uniquely human: *revenge*. You will have to decide for yourself why the playwright chooses to emphasize the reactions he does.

Tubal, a friend of Shylock's and fellow Jew, arrives bearing both welcome and unwelcome news. Another of Antonio's ships has been lost near Tripolis and his creditors are predicting that he will be forced to "break"—that is, declare bankruptcy.

Tubal also reports that Jessica and Lorenzo have been seen in Genoa where she spent fourscore (eighty) ducats in one night and sold one of Shylock's rings to buy a pet monkey.

Shylock gloats over Antonio's bad luck and curses his daughter for stealing his money and jewels. "I would my daughter were dead at my foot, and the jewels in her ear," he says angrily. His reaction to the news that Jessica has sold his turquoise ring is more likely to touch our sympathies. The ring, Shylock recalls, was a gift from Leah (presumably his dead wife) before his marriage. "I would not have given it for a wilderness of monkeys" he sighs.

NOTE: What do you think about Jessica's behavior? It may be difficult to forgive a daughter who would steal her father's money and then spend it on silly extravagances, like a pet monkey. Elizabethan audiences probably felt, on the other hand, that there was no more appropriate punishment for a miser than to have a child who turns out to be a spendthrift. Whether you agree or not depends on whether you find yourself identifying with Shylock or with his rebellious daughter.

ACT III, SCENE II

Bassanio is in Belmont, ready to try his luck with the test of the three caskets. It is obvious that Bassanio and Portia have fallen in love. She begs him to put off the test for a few days so that they can enjoy each other's company, and declares that if it weren't for her sworn promise, she would be happy to tell him which casket is the right one. Bassanio insists on going through with the test right away. The suspense is torture, he says. He feels as if he were "on the rack."

Portia calls for music to be played before Bassanio makes his choice, explaining that music is an appropriate accompaniment to both joyous occasions and sad ones.

The lyrics to the song Portia calls for are:

> Tell me where is fancy bred,
> Or in the heart, or in the head?
> How begot, how nourished?
>   Reply, reply.
> It is engend'red in the eyes,
> With gazing fed, and fancy dies
> In the cradle where it lies.

NOTE: Fancy is a superficial attraction, in the sense of "taking a fancy" to someone or something. The song, then, says that fancy begins in the eyes—not the heart or the head. It also dies there. The word 'lie' has a double meaning, suggesting both that fancy lies in its "cradle" (the eyes) and that it is deceiving.

Is Portia giving Bassanio a hint after all? Many readers think so. Notice that the first lines of this song—bred, head and nourish'*ed*—all rhyme with lead, the casket which we know, by the process of elimination, must be the right one. The song is also a warning against trusting the inclinations of one's eyes—which would naturally tempt a suitor to choose the more beautiful and valuable-looking chests.

Other readers insist just as strongly that it would be against Portia's character for her to break the rules of her father's will by telling Bassanio the right answer. What do you think?

Debating his choice, Bassanio notes that outward appearances can be deceiving. Vice can be made to look like virtue. Beauty cannot be evaluated by weight like other commodities, since those who have the most of it are often the "lightest." (Light, in Elizabethan English meant morally loose and unchaste, as well as light in weight.) Bassanio calls gold "hard food for Midas"—recalling the myth of how Midas starved after he got his wish that everything he touched would turn to gold. And he dismisses silver as a "common drudge"—the everyday medium of exchange in business. Thus, by a process of elimination, he chooses the lead casket, explaining that its "plainess moves me more than eloquence."

NOTE: In some editions of the play you will find the word "paleness" in place of "plainess." Most scholars nowadays agree that "plainess" is the word Shakespeare originally used. "Paleness" is a characteristic of silver.

Of course, we already know that Bassanio has made the correct choice. But what about Bassanio's reasons for settling on it? Do they surprise you? Some readers have objected that Bassanio has so far not seemed to be the type of person who looks beneath surface appearances. Also, his speech might seem more appropriate in a story such as *Cinderella*, where the inner beauty of the heroine is not immediately apparent. In Portia's case there is no discrepancy between external appearance and inner worth; she is as beautiful and rich as she is virtuous! Why should her portrait be in the lead casket?

On the other hand, you will recall from Act II, Scene VII that the motto on the lead casket read: "Who chooseth me must give and hazard all he hath." Unlike Portia's previous suitors, Bassanio is neither too proud nor too cautious to mind taking risks. We have already learned this about him—even though, as some readers point out, it is Antonio who has risked the most. The scene does not tell us that external beauty and true worth *never* go together. What it does seem to be saying is that you will never find the hidden joys of true love unless you are willing to take chances. The most obvious difference between Bassanio and the other suitors is that he is in love. He has risked offering his heart to Portia.

Portia, of course, is overjoyed by Bassanio's choice. For his sake, she says, she can only wish that she were even richer and more beautiful than she is. "What is mine is yours" she declares. As a token of her pledge, she gives Bassanio a ring, cautioning him that if he ever loses it or gives it away it will be a sign that their love is about to end.

NOTE: The language that Portia uses in pledging herself to Bassanio accentuates the play's theme of love as a form of wealth. Describing herself, Portia sounds almost like an accountant reading a balance sheet. She talks of the "sum" of her virtues and hopes that they will "exceed account." In wishing that she could increase her beauty and her fortune, she calls to mind the way that money multiplies by earning interest.

After congratulating the lovers, Gratiano and Nerissa make an announcement of their own: They, too, have fallen in love, and before the test of the caskets Nerissa had vowed that if Bassanio won Portia, she would marry Gratiano. Bassanio agrees that the two couples should get married in a double ceremony.

At this moment, Salerio, Lorenzo and Jessica arrive with a letter from Antonio. All of Antonio's ships have been lost, he is broke, and he is unable to repay the loan to Shylock. Since making good on his "bond"—the promised pound of flesh—is sure to cost him his life, he is writing to forgive all Bassanio's debts to him. He begs, however, that for the sake of their friendship, Bassanio come back to Venice to see him one last time before he dies.

Bassanio is deeply moved by his friend's troubles and is guilt-stricken for being the one who has endangered Antonio's life. Portia immediately urges Bassanio to go back to Venice and repay the loan with her money. Offer Shylock twice what he has coming to him, she says, even twenty times as much, whatever it will take to satisfy him.

The two couples hurry off to the church to be married. Afterward Bassanio and Gratiano leave immediately with Salerio for Venice.

ACT III, SCENE III

Back in Venice, Antonio has been allowed to leave his jail cell long enough to go to Shylock and plead for mercy. Antonio is accompanied by his jailer and his friend Solanio. Shylock, however, refuses even to listen to what Antonio has to say. You called me a dog, Shylock reminds Antonio. Well, since I'm a dog, "beware my fangs."

After Shylock leaves, Antonio comments to Solanio that he knows why Shylock hates him. On many occasions, he has helped out friends who would otherwise have lost their property to the moneylender, in forfeit for unpaid debts. Solanio remarks that the Duke, the ruler of Venice, will surely never force Antonio to pay this particular forfeiture. Antonio disagrees. If the Duke does not uphold the law, he says, he will undermine the reputation of Venice and that could influence foreigners against doing business there. For the sake of commerce, a bona fide contract must be upheld.

Antonio adds that he has given up all hope, and he jokes bitterly that he has lost so much weight from worry that he may not have a pound of flesh left tomorrow when Shylock is due to collect on the bond.

ACT III, SCENE IV

The scene now shifts back to Belmont where we find Lorenzo praising Portia for sending Bassanio on his errand of mercy.

"I never did repent for doing good," Portia answers. Since Antonio is a dear friend of her "lord" Bassanio, she adds, then he might as well be her lord, too. She will do anything she can to help him.

In the meantime, Portia tells Lorenzo, she and Nerissa have made a vow to go into retreat where they will pray and meditate until their husbands' safe return. She asks Lorenzo and Jessica to stay in Belmont and look after her house until she returns.

Portia then calls aside her servant Balthasar and orders him to deliver a letter to her cousin Bellario, a doctor of law in Padua. Bellario will give Balthasar some paper and clothing which he is to take straight to Venice, where Portia will meet him by the public ferry.

Balthasar leaves on his errand and Portia, now alone with Nerissa, confides that she has a secret plan. The two women are going to dress up as men and go to Venice to help Antonio. Portia boasts about what a fine young man she will make. She knows all the tricks of the "bragging Jacks" who lie about their success with women, she says.

Portia promises Nerissa that once they are in

their coach on the road to Venice, she will explain the rest of her plan.

ACT III, SCENE V

In the garden of Portia's house in Belmont, Launcelot is teasing Jessica, telling her that he is afraid she will be damned because her father is a Jew. Her only hope of being saved, he goes on, is that Shylock is not really her father. Jessica reminds Launcelot that she has converted to Christianity since her marriage to Lorenzo.

At the end of the scene, Jessica and Lorenzo discuss their high opinion of Portia. Their conversation seems less important for its subject than for what it shows us about the relationship between the two lovers. Whatever we may have thought of Jessica previously, this scene shows her to be warm-hearted, tender and in love with her husband. Some readers feel that the playwright is showing us that Jessica has mellowed since her marriage and her exposure to the serenity of Belmont. Others feel that this scene is intended merely as a light, entertaining interlude which gives the audience a chance to catch its breath before the important business that will take place in Act IV.

ACT IV
ACT IV, SCENE I

Lines 1–121
The Duke of Venice is about to hold a hearing to decide whether or not Shylock can legally collect his pound of flesh from Antonio. There is no question of where the Duke's sympathies lie. Before

the hearing gets under way, he tells Antonio and his friends that he has already tried, without success, to talk Shylock into showing mercy. When Shylock appears in the court, the Duke once again lectures him, declaring that Antonio's plight would win mercy even from "brassy bosoms and hearts of rough flint," from "Turks and Tartars."

Shylock, however, insists that he only wants what is legally his. His reasons for desiring Antonio's flesh may be unfair, but this is his "humor"—his whim—and he is entitled to satisfy it. Bassanio interrupts to repeat that he is willing to repay the principal of the loan several times over, but Shylock scorns the offer.

When the Duke reproves Shylock once again for not showing mercy, Shylock defends himself rather cleverly. You Christians own slaves, he says. What would you say if I urged you to let them go for the sake of showing mercy? No doubt you would say, "The slaves are ours."

Many playgoers find themselves at least partially in sympathy with Shylock at this point. After all, he is correct in drawing attention to the double standard of morality that the Duke and the other Venetian Christians live by. Would any of them be so interested in mercy if it weren't one of their own friends whose life was at stake? Perhaps not. Others point out that Shylock is resorting to a common trick for escaping blame for one's own actions. There is always evil and hypocrisy in the world, but some people never take much interest in denouncing it until they need an excuse to draw attention away from their own bad deeds. What examples of this kind of rationalization that you have encountered in your own experience can you offer?

Lines 122–250

Just when the argument seems to have reached an impasse, the Duke announces that a messenger has arrived with a letter from the learned Bellario of Padua. The messenger, who is actually Nerissa disguised as a page boy, enters and gives the letter to the Duke. Bellario's message informs the court that he is very interested in Antonio's case, but since he is too ill to come to Venice himself he has sent Balthasar, a young but very learned doctor of laws, to give an opinion on his behalf.

NOTE: There are a number of improbable coincidences in the play, beginning with Antonio's sudden run of bad luck, just when he has pledged his own body to guarantee Bassanio's loan. That the Duke just happens to have written to Doctor Bellario, Portia's cousin, for an opinion on the case is another. Most likely, Shakespeare's audiences would have accepted this particular coincidence as plausible because Padua was the site of a very famous university in Renaissance Italy. Thus, calling in a legal expert from Padua would be equivalent to getting an opinion from a Harvard Law School professor today.

While the Duke is reading the letter from Doctor Bellario, Shylock, confident of victory, is already sharpening the knife that he will use to cut out Antonio's heart. Gratiano, seeing this, accuses him of having the soul of a dog.

The young doctor of laws "Balthasar" is Portia, disguised as a young man. From the moment Portia comes on stage in this scene (usually costumed in the flowing robes of a Renaissance doctor of laws) she holds everyone's full attention. Naturally, no one recognizes her, not even her newlywed husband, Bassanio. (It's a stage tradition which we accept.)

Portia announces almost immediately that she has found nothing in Venetian law that would disallow Shylock's "strange suit." Therefore, it is up to him to show mercy. Although the Duke has already argued for mercy in his own way, Portia's speech is far more eloquent:

> The quality of mercy is not strained,
> It droppeth as the gentle rain from heaven
> Upon the place beneath. It is twice blest—
> It blesseth him that gives, and him that takes.

In essence, Portia is saying that one does not need a reason for showing mercy. The virtue of mercy lies in its being given freely, without constraint—just as God allows the rain to fall on the just and the unjust alike. Moreover, mercy is a blessing to the giver, not just to the person who directly benefits from it.

Portia goes on to say that mercy is an attribute of God himself. This, she points out, is fortunate, since if God's justice were not tempered by mercy none of us would ever "see salvation."

Shylock is unmoved by this argument. "I crave the law," he insists gruffly.

If that is so, Portia agrees, then there in no power in Venice that can keep him from collecting his bond!

NOTE: Shylock, overjoyed at his apparent victory, calls Portia a "Daniel." This is a reference not to the story of Daniel in the Old Testament, but to the apocryphal Old Testament "Book of Daniel" which is no longer included in many modern-day Bibles. In this book, a young woman named Susanna rejects the advances of two important men, and they seek revenge by accusing her of adultery with someone else. Daniel, a very youthful judge, cleverly proves that the accusation is a lie. Anyone who knows this particular story would have to suspect, at this point, that Shylock is celebrating too soon. Daniel's judgment, after all, saved an innocent party from becoming the victim of mean-spirited revenge. If Portia truly is a "Daniel," then Shylock is definitely in trouble.

Lines 251–344

For the moment, Portia seems about to let Shylock triumph. She orders Antonio to bare his chest for Shylock's knife. She even asks whether Shylock has a scale on hand, so that he can weigh the flesh that he cuts from Antonio's body. Shylock, completely prepared to carry out his grisly plan, proudly announces that he does have one. Then, almost as an afterthought, Portia wonders whether Shylock has a surgeon on hand to stop Antonio from bleeding to death.

Shylock is taken aback. The terms of the contract didn't say anything about a surgeon, he reminds Portia.

Will Shylock be allowed to go ahead and cut out Antonio's heart? Or does Portia have a last trick in reserve that will stop him?

The most suspenseful moment of the play has arrived. Even so, the author still takes time out for a bit of wry humor. Antonio, convinced that he is going to die, exchanges tearful farewells with his friends. In their grief, both Bassanio and Gratiano vow that they would sacrifice anything, even their beloved wives, if it could save Antonio's life. As you can imagine, neither "Balthasar" nor his "page" are particularly pleased to hear this. Both remark on how displeased the gentlemen's wives would be if they were only around to hear these remarks.

In the meantime, Portia pretends that she has discovered something in the fine print of the court papers that had escaped her notice before. "Tarry a little," she says. The agreement doesn't say anything about Shylock being entitled to Antonio's blood. Therefore, Shylock can have his pound of flesh—*but* only if he can take it without shedding so much as a drop of Antonio's blood!

Shylock realizes at once that he has been outwitted. He immediately begs to be allowed to take the 9000 ducats Bassanio had offered and leave. But Portia has one more surprise in store. There is a law on the books in Venice which says that it is a capital crime for any alien (which includes Shylock as a Jew) to plot against the life of a citizen. Shylock, of course, has been doing exactly that. If the Duke wishes to interpret the law literally, Shylock could be sentenced to hang.

NOTE: There are always a few readers who feel that Portia's victory in court comes a little too easily. One critic has even complained that Portia wins through a mere legal "quibble." Others contend that the Duke and even Shylock would surely have known about such a law if it existed. The latter argument may be true, although Shylock would not be the first to become careless about such details in the rush to get revenge on an enemy.

These objections overlook the reasons why most playgoers, and most readers too, enjoy court scenes. The fear of ending up in court, as the hapless victim of a lawsuit or the defendant wrongly accused, is a very common one. Many people feel that the law is really an artificial game of wits in any case. They enjoy seeing a clever advocate win the case on behalf of an endangered hero, whether or not the case is won on the basis of an argument that is a mere "quibble."

On a less literal level, we may suspect Antonio's fate in court has little to do with legal arguments. The gist of Portia's famous speech about mercy is that justice without mercy is not true justice at all. This is a philosophical and religious argument, not, strictly speaking, a legal one. By winning her case, Portia seems to confirm the belief that the law is also merciful in real life. Do you think that this is true?

Lines 345–422

Now it is Shylock's turn to beg for mercy. It is interesting to see how the other characters respond to this turnabout.

Gratiano, who prides himself on being so happy-go-lucky, gloats over Shylock's plight and suggests that he ought to go home and hang himself to save the government the price of the rope.

The Duke rules that Shylock's life will be spared, but his fortune will go half to the state and half to Antonio. The state's share, he hints, may even be reduced to a mere fine.

Antonio, in turn, adds that if the Duke will be satisfied with a fine, he will agree to keep his half of Shylock's goods in stewardship for Shylock's son-in-law Lorenzo, so that after Shylock's death he will have an inheritance. However, Antonio also adds two other stipulations: First, Shylock must agree to leave the rest of his goods in his will to Lorenzo and Jessica. Second, he must promise to convert to Christianity.

To all this, Shylock answers simply: "I am content."

NOTE: Do you believe that Shylock is being sincere? Or are these the words of a bitter, defeated man who has no other choice?

In thinking about your answer, keep in mind that Elizabethans believed that only Christians had a chance of entering heaven. So getting someone to convert, even by force, was doing him a favor. Also, we are led to think that Shylock still has plenty of money left. Certainly, if Shakespeare had wanted to stress Shylock's humiliation, he could have made his punishment much worse. At the very least, he could have made him grovel and beg for his life, but he does not. Considering what *might* have happened, Shylock may well have good reason to feel content.

On the other hand, if you go to see a production of *The Merchant of Venice* today, you will probably find that the actor playing Shylock delivers this line with a good deal of irony. Many modern readers can't help feeling that there is something wrong with a conception of mercy which is not broad enough to accommodate an adversary's right to his own religion. Also, notice that even when the Duke and Portia have invited Antonio to show mercy to Shylock, Antonio still seems to be concerned more with getting an inheritance for *his* friend Lorenzo than with being merciful to the moneylender. After

all he has been through, Antonio is still oblivious
to the possibility that he might bear some responsibility for turning Shylock against him. You will
have to decide for yourself whether this seems fair
within the context of the play.

Lines 423–472

After Shylock and the Duke have departed, Bassanio thanks the young lawyer and offers to reward "him" generously for saving Antonio's life.
Portia refuses to take any money, but she asks Bassanio to give her his ring as a token to remember
the occasion by. Bassanio doesn't know what to
do. He begs the "lawyer" to accept another ring
in its place. He will gladly buy the good doctor the
most expensive ring in Venice. For the ring he is
wearing, he says, was a present from his wife, and
he has made a vow never to part with it.

Portia pretends to consider this just a lame excuse. If your wife is not a "madwoman," she says,
she would understand the circumstances and forgive you.

After the "lawyer" has left, Antonio persuades
Bassanio to give up the ring for his sake. Bassanio
cannot bring himself to refuse his friend at this
moment, so he asks Gratiano to hurry after the
lawyer and deliver the ring as a gift.

ACT IV, SCENE II

Gratiano catches up with Portia and gives her
the ring. Portia accepts the gift, and she asks Gratiano to take her "page boy" to Shylock's house.
As they prepare to leave, Portia whispers to Ne-

rissa that she should do her best to make Gratiano give up *his* ring to her.

This brief scene makes it obvious that Portia and her maid are looking forward to confronting their husbands about the rings later on.

ACT V
ACT V, SCENE I

In Belmont, Lorenzo and Jessica are happily exchanging vows of love on a moonlit night. A messenger breaks in on their conversation to announce that Portia will be returning to the house before morning. No sooner does he finish speaking than Launcelot the clown brings similar news about Bassanio.

Lorenzo calls for the house musicians to come outdoors and play so that he and Jessica can enjoy their music and the moonlight while waiting for Portia and Bassanio's return. "How sweet the moonlight sleeps upon this bank!" says Lorenzo:

> Here we will sit and let the sounds of music
> Creep in our ears; soft stillness and the night
> Become the touches of sweet harmony.

NOTE: Lorenzo's speech about music here is worth studying carefully. Not only does it contain some of the most beautiful language of the play, but it expresses the play's overall view of the importance of harmony. The harmony of music is mirrored in the sought-after harmony of social relationships. When Jessica interrupts her husband's speech to comment that music never makes her merry, Lorenzo says that this is because Jessica is a good listener. Music does not exist, he says,

merely to entertain the "wild and wanton herd."
At the same time, the person who has no music
in him is not to be trusted. The virtue of music, in
Lorenzo's opinion, is its "sweetness," its moder-
ating influence on the extremes of human passion.
(At this point, you may also recall Nerissa's earlier
comment that extreme wealth, like extreme pov-
erty, can be a cause of unhappiness. Lorenzo is
going a step farther, arguing that true happiness
is also found in emotional moderation, not abrupt
swings of mood.)

Portia and Nerissa reach the house while the
music is still playing and, characteristically, Portia
has a few thoughts on the subject of music that
are more wry than Lorenzo's sweet meditation.
She observes that the effect of music has a good
deal to do with the setting in which we hear it.
When no one is around to hear him, she suggests,
the crow probably sings as sweetly as the lark.
Moreover, if nightingales sang by day instead of
under the moonlight, no one would think their
song was especially beautiful.

At first, Portia's remarks may seem to contradict
Lorenzo's. Notice, though, that in her way Portia,
too, is advocating balance and harmony. Beauty of
any kind does not exist for its own sake, she seems
to be saying. It can be enjoyed only in the appropriate setting and season.

Just as the first light of dawn breaks, Bassanio
appears at the house, accompanied by Gratiano
and Antonio. As you might expect, it does not take
long for Portia and Nerissa to discover that their
husbands are no longer wearing their rings. Bas-

sanio and Gratiano try to explain how they had no choice but to give the rings away. However, Portia and Nerissa refuse to accept their husbands' story that the rings were given to two men. They insist indignantly that the rings were really given to *women*—and, of course, they are right although Bassanio and Gratiano do not realize it.

Shifting tactics, Portia next declares that if the young "doctor" who has the ring ever shows up at her house, she will be just as generous to him as Bassanio was. She'll deny him nothing. She will even sleep with him!

At this, Antonio interrupts and tries to explain that it was his fault that Bassanio gave away the ring. He talked him into parting with it.

Very well, says Portia, then give him this, and make sure he takes better care of it than the last present he had from me. The ring that Portia hands to Antonio is, naturally, the same ring that Bassanio gave her when he thought that she was Balthasar the lawyer. Bassanio recognizes the ring and is completely confused. How did Portia get it back? I got it, says Portia, by sleeping with the "doctor" Balthasar. Nerissa now chimes in and says that she spent last night in bed with Balthasar's page.

Having taken her joke to its limit, Portia at last gives in and tells Bassanio the truth. She *was* Balthasar, the clever doctor of laws who saved Antonio's life. Antonio is dumbfounded by this revelation. Bassanio, on his part, passes quickly from surprise to open admiration of his wife's clever resourcefulness. Instead of being miffed—as he might be at being left in ignorance of the plan—he is clearly charmed, and even more in love with Portia than he was before.

NOTE: Considering how much this play has to say about the need for loyalty in love and friendship, you might be surprised at how lightly the men take Portia and Nerissa's teasing claim to have slept with other men. Gratiano's reaction to hearing his bride say that she has already enjoyed a lover on the side is not outrage but bemusement. He complains, not that he has been betrayed, but that he has been betrayed so soon. Gratiano is even given the very last line of the play, which he turns into a dirty joke by vowing that from now on he will keep safe "Nerissa's ring"—a bawdy reference to the female genitalia. Gratiano's remarks—indeed the whole episode of the rings—reinforce the play's lighthearted mood. While we don't seriously expect these lovers to be unfaithful to each other in the future, we also sense that they will remain true out of continuing affection for each other, not because they are overly conscientious about the strictures of oaths and marriage vows.

Portia has one last piece of good news to relate. She has a letter for Antonio informing him that by some "strange accident" three of his ships, which were supposedly wrecked, have returned to port safely.

With this development, the action of the play has come full circle. The lovers are happily united, and Antonio is a wealthy man again.

Despite its lighthearted mood, this final scene is a rather unusual conclusion for a romantic comedy. While the supporting characters have found love and happiness, Antonio—the play's hero—is left alone, a temporary guest in the domestic uto-

pia of Belmont. Antonio's fate is particularly strik-
ing if you compare the ending of *The Merchant of
Venice* with the conclusion of other Shakespearean
comedies such as *Comedy of Errors*, *Two Gentlemen
of Verona*, and *Twelfth Night*, in which pairs of friends
or siblings are neatly matched up with lovers of
the opposite sex. If *The Merchant of Venice* followed
this pattern, we would expect to find Antonio, not
the lightweight Gratiano, married to Nerissa. One
reason for this ending may be simply that Antonio
has hardly had time to go courting. Nevertheless,
one can't help but notice that Antonio, the most
generous character in the play, remains the most
alone. His situation adds a melancholy note to the
cheerful final chord of this composition—recalling
the play's theme that the greatest music is not necessarily the most light and carefree.

As a practical matter, Antonio's fate poses a
problem for the directors of stage productions of
the play. Some directors choose to end this scene
with Portia, Bassanio, and Antonio entering Portia's house together—a grouping which emphasizes the enduring bonds of their friendship. Other
directors emphasize Antonio's situation as an outsider. One recent television production concluded
with the newlyweds rushing happily off to bed
while Antonio stands forlornly on the doorstep of
the house. If you were staging a production of *The
Merchant of Venice*, how would you direct your actors to behave at the end of this scene?

A STEP BEYOND

Tests and Answers
TESTS

Test 1

1. In this play music and musical imagery _____
   A. create a mood of joyful abandon
   B. signal abrupt switches in emotional tone
   C. emphasize the value of harmony

2. "It's a wise father who knows his own child" is said by _____
   A. Jessica   B. Launcelot
   C. Lorenzo

3. The young Venetians like to compare themselves to _____
   A. merchant ships
   B. unrefined gold
   C. musical instruments

4. The episode of the rings might be said to show _____
   A. that Bassanio does not take his marriage seriously
   B. that loyalty in spirit is more important than vows and sworn oaths
   C. that Bassanio will eventually have to choose between his best friend and his wife

5. In joking about her German suitor, Portia suggests _____

   A. placing a bottle of wine on the wrong
      casket
   B. he's in love with his horse
   C. he's a vile coward

6. Hanging and wiving are said to be alike   _____
   because
   A. wise men avoid both
   B. both last forever
   C. both are determined by fate

7. "The shadowed livery of the burnished sun"   _____
   refers to
   A. the new uniform Bassanio gives
      Launcelot
   B. the Prince of Morocco's complexion
   C. Shylock's hoarded gold

8. The casket picked by the Prince of Arragon   _____
   is the wrong one because
   A. silver is less valuable than gold
   B. his choice was too obvious
   C. his choice was dictated by logic, not
      love

9. The song "Tell me where is fancy bred"   _____
   says that
   A. unlike true love, fancy can be
      deceiving
   B. good breeding always shows in the
      end
   C. love at first sight is the best kind of
      love

10. Shylock hates Antonio because   _____
   I. he is a Christian
   II. he has insulted him

III. he deals in merchandise
IV. he lends money without charging
    interest
A. II only   B. I and III only
C. all of these
D. I, II and IV only

11. What does *The Merchant of Venice* have to say about
the relationship between love and wealth?

12. Most of the Italian cities mentioned in Shakespeare's
plays are so vaguely described that they are virtually
interchangeable. Venice is an exception. What does
this play tell us about Venice and its people?

13. Is Shylock a comic character or a tragic one? Discuss.

14. Discuss the role of humor in *The Merchant of Venice.*

Test 2

1. In *The Merchant of Venice,* love and money   _____
   are
   A. enjoyed only by those who guard
      them carefully
   B. two forms of wealth
   C. in constant conflict

2. "The quality of mercy is not strained" means   _____
   A. mercy is given freely, without
      constraint
   B. mercy should be given only when it
      puts no strain on the giver
   C. the good and bad aspects of mercy are
      hard to separate

3. "Love is blind" refers to   _____
   A. the test of the three caskets
   B. Jessica's disguise

   C. Bassanio's failure to recognize Portia
      when she is dressed as a man

4. The lead casket is the right choice because   ____
   A. lead symbolizes seriousness and
      weighty thoughts
   B. to find true love you have to be
      willing to take risks
   C. great beauty and inner worth never
      go together

5. Tubal added to Shylock's woes by telling   ____
   him
   A. how Jessica squandered his money
   B. that Antonio's ships were coming
      safely to port
   C. that the Duke would not honor his
      contract

6. One sign of Gratiano's excessive wildness   ____
   is his
   A. running off to Belmont
   B. hasty marriage to Nerissa
   C. fondness for dirty puns

7. Nerissa says that it is easiest to be happy   ____
   if you are
   A. average   B. married   C. rich

8. The reason that Portia's father set up the   ____
   test of the caskets is that
   A. Portia might have married a fortune
      hunter otherwise
   B. he wanted his daughter to have a
      wise husband
   C. never told to us in the play

9. Antonio pledges a pound of his own flesh   ____
   because

A. he is a good and generous friend
B. he refuses to pay usury
C. he knows the law will never allow Shylock to collect

10. In the trial scene, "I am content" is said by _____
    A. Bassanio   B. Shylock   C. Portia

11. Is Bassanio's speech about appearance versus inner worth at the time he chooses the lead casket consistent with what we know about his character? Why or why not?

12. How are music and musical imagery used throughout the play?

13. What is the significance of the episode of the rings?

14. What does the play have to say about the relationship between friendship and love?

ANSWERS

Test 1

1. C   **2.** B   **3.** A   **4.** B   **5.** A   **6.** C
7. B   **8.** C   **9.** A   **10.** D

11. Love and money are closely intertwined in this play. By winning Portia, Bassanio solves his romantic problems and his financial ones simultaneously. Shylock, on the other hand, loses both his daughter Jessica and his ducats. Antonio demonstrates his friendship by lending money freely—even to the point of pledging his own flesh to guarantee the loan that Shylock extends to Bassanio. The very language that is used to describe human relationship underlines the theme of love as a form of wealth. Portia, declaring her love for Bassanio, describes herself in terms that recall a financial balance sheet—for example, she tells Bassanio that she wishes to stand high in his "account." Salerio and Solanio also use language which compares the progress of a person's life to the quest for profit through trade on the high seas. Other connections between love and wealth include the use of the gold rings which symbolize the vows exchanged by Portia and Bassanio, Nerissa and Gratiano. Finally, the test of the three caskets turns on a contrast between outward appearances and inner worth.

12. Venice is portrayed as a rich and cosmopolitan city, a busy seaport engaged in trade with exotic foreign lands. Although there is very little physical description of Venice, the behavior of Antonio and his friends tell us a good deal about Venetian life—or, at least, about Shakespeare's conception of it. These young men cheerfully live beyond their means, confident that money will come their way sooner or later. Bassanio, although he has just borrowed a large sum of money on his friend's credit, is not at all worried about keeping his expenses down— he plans to celebrate his departure for Belmont by holding a dinner party and a masque. Note, also, that most of the Venetian scenes take place in the street or in public places; the choice of settings emphasizes the importance of business and civic activities in the lives of the Venetians. Shylock is the only character we see at home, and his attachment to his house is offered as evidence of his gloomy, miserly personality. The trial scene further emphasizes that the Venetians' respect for law is related to their desire to assure foreigners that they will be treated fairly in business.

13. The part of Shylock has been played both ways over the centuries. Most Shakespeare scholars agree that the part of Shylock was written as a comic villain; however, modern actors are more likely to stress the serious side to Shylock's character. Whichever way you choose to answer this question, you should keep in mind that calling Shylock a comic character does not necessarily mean that his actions constantly provoke laughter. If you believe, for example, that sheer greed is the most important motivation for Shylock's plotting—and that he learns his lesson during the trial scene and has reason to accept the verdict against him as basically merciful, then you can justify seeing Shylock as the villain in a comedy. If you believe that Shylock suffers largely because he is an outsider and that his final line in the play is bitterly ironic, then you cannot help seeing him as a tragic figure.

14. In answering this question, you might choose to concentrate on the role of Launcelot, the clown. Launcelot's humor is based on his mangled vocabulary—a mixture of mispronounced words and silly puns—as well as on broad physical comedy. You might note, also, that while Launcelot's speeches are sheer silliness, they do echo some of the serious issues raised in the play—particularly Jessica's relationship to her father Shylock. Another form of humor is the more literate, though sometimes off-color, kind of pun which Gratiano specializes in. Gratiano's character provides an excuse for Shakespeare to indulge in this form of humor, while at the same time having other characters in the play gently reprove Gratiano for his bad taste. The protagonists of the play enjoy humor—Bassanio even hires Launcelot as a servant. But we are given to believe that extreme levity is a fault. The truly happy person does not have to be constantly cracking jokes.

Test 2

1. B	2. A	3. B	4. B	5. A	6. C
7. A	8. C	9. A	10. B		

11. Many readers feel that Bassanio's speech is out of character. Suddenly this charming spendthrift comes out with a philosophical meditation on the superficial nature of external wealth and beauty! On the other hand, if you think of the mottos inscribed on the various caskets—which are mentioned earlier during the scene with the Prince of Morocco—then Bassanio's choice is not out of character. It would be just like him to choose "hazard"—or chance—over a sure thing. In considering this question further, you might also ask yourself whether readers who find Bassanio frivolous in the early scenes of the play do him an injustice. After all, Bassanio does express concern for Antonio and wants to pay back the money he owes. Depending on your interpretations of Bassanio's speeches—and on your own views of friendship and financial responsibility—it is possible to defend differing opinions of Bassanio's character.

12. In discussing the role of music in the play, you should be sure to mention Portia's comments on music in Act III, Scene II as well as what she and Lorenzo say about music as the bringer of harmony in Act V. In the latter section of the play, you will recall, Lorenzo says that the man who has no feeling for music is not to be trusted—a comment that recalls Shylock's desire to shut the music of the masque out of his house. Lorenzo also says that music exists not so much to make us carefree and happy as to induce contemplation and thoughtfulness—and this is certainly the effect that the song "Tell Me Where is Fancy Bred" has on Bassanio in Act III, Scene II.

13. Readers who stress that the action of the play is circular tend to see the episode of the rings as symbolizing this circularity. Portia gives her ring to Bassanio, who gives it back to her thinking she is the lawyer Balthasar; she later gives the ring to Antonio who hands it back to Bassanio again. All of these exchanges together might be seen as emphasizing the play's theme that love only increases in power if it is given freely. Another way of looking at the rings is that they represent a gentle, loving bond between human beings—as opposed to the cruel bond (or promise) imposed on Antonio by Shylock. Either way, the important feature of the episode of the rings is that Bassanio is not punished for breaking his vow never to part with the token of Portia's love. In a tragedy, breaking such a promise would surely have terrible consequences. In this play, it becomes an occasion for some playful teasing but no serious repercussions.

14. *The Merchant of Venice* tells us that love and friendship are thoroughly compatible. Far from being jealous of her husband's friendship with Antonio, Portia says that "the bosom lover of my lord / must needs be like my lord." Portia not only saves Antonio's life, but at the end of the play Antonio is brought back to Belmont to share in the happy final scene. This, at least, is what the play says on its surface. Some readers, however, feel that there is a conflict between love and friendship expressed on a deeper level. These readers stress that Antonio, despite his brief visit to Belmont, cannot stay there long; he is shut out, without a bride of his own, and must return almost immediately to Venice.

Term Paper Ideas and other Topics for Writing

The Play

1. Choose one of the following interpretations and discuss:

    a. *The Merchant of Venice* is a problem play about the question of usury.

b. *The Merchant of Venice* is a light romantic comedy which was never intended as a comment on important social issues.

c. *The Merchant of Venice* contrasts the Old Testament view of God as law-giver with the New Testament view of God as offering salvation through divine mercy.

d. Considering the times during which it was written, *The Merchant of Venice* expresses humane and tolerant values.

e. *The Merchant of Venice* is an outdated play because it is a comedy based on assumptions which we today find unacceptable.

2. Discuss the concept of harmony as presented in the play. Does this concept have any application to real life? Or does it make sense only in the unrealistically benign world of this play?

3. What is the attitude towards money and its uses in the play? How does it compare with modern-day attitudes?

4. How does Shakespeare weave together the stories of the "pound of flesh" and the "three caskets"?

The Characters

1. Defend or attack the view that Bassanio is nothing but a fortune hunter.

2. Can you see any similarities between the characters of Antonio and Shylock? If so, what are they?

3. Contrast the characters of Gratiano and Shylock. In what ways are they opposites?

4. What function do Salerio and Solanio serve in the play?

5. Did Portia give Bassanio a clue to the choice of the

correct casket? How would such behavior affect your view of her character?

6. Discuss how Shakespeare establishes Shylock's position as an outsider.

Miscellaneous

1. Choose one of the following types of imagery and discuss its use in the play:

- a. ships and the sea
- b. gold
- c. music
- d. money lent at interest

2. As an exercise, rewrite one or more scenes of the play in the form of a story or prose sketch. Take the point of view of Shylock, of Portia, or of Bassanio.

3. The critic E. M. W. Tillyard wrote: "Shakespeare's Shylock has been the victim of the great actor." Discuss. If possible, consult a stage history such as Toby Lelyveld's *Shylock on the Stage*.

4. If you could direct a production of *The Merchant of Venice*, how would you go about interpreting the trial scene? . . . Or, the final moments of Act V?

Further Reading
CRITICAL WORKS

Auden, W. H. "Love and Usury in *The Merchant of Venice*." In *Four Centuries of Shakespeare Criticism*, ed. by Frank Kermode. New York: Avon, 1965.

Charlton, H. B. *Shakespearean Comedy*. New York: Methuen, 1938. A sympathetic view of Shylock.

Danson, Lawrence. *The Harmonies of The Merchant of Venice*. New Haven: Yale University Press, 1978.

Grebanier, Bernard. *The Truth About Shylock*. New York: Random House, 1962.

Holland, Norman. *The Shakespearean Imagination*. New York: Macmillan, 1964.

Lelyveld, Toby. *Shylock on the Stage*. London: Routledge, 1961.

Sinsheimer, Hermann. *Shylock*. New York: Benjamin Blom, 1947. Includes much historical background on usury and Jews in medieval and Renaissance literature.

Tillyard, E. M. W. *Shakespeare's Early Comedies*. New York: Barnes & Noble, 1965.

Van Doren, Mark. *Shakespeare*. New York: Henry Holt, 1939.

Walley, Harold. "Shakespeare's Portrayal of Shylock." *The Parrott Presentation Volume*, ed. Hardin Craig. New York: Russell & Russell, 1967.

Weiss, Theodore. *The Breath of Clowns and Kings: Shakespeare's Early Comedies and Histories*. New York: Atheneum, 1971.

Wilders, John, ed. *The Merchant of Venice: A Selection of Critical Essays*. London: Macmillan, 1969. Criticism from 1709 to 1963, including many of the more important essays on the play.

AUTHOR'S WORKS

Shakespeare wrote 37 plays (38 if you include *The Two Noble Kinsmen*) over a 20-year period, from about 1590 to 1610. It's difficult to determine the exact dates when many were written, but scholars have made the following intelligent guesses about his plays and poems:

Plays

1588–93	*The Comedy of Errors*
1588–94	*Love's Labor's Lost*
1590–91	*2 Henry VI*
1590–91	*3 Henry VI*
1591–92	*1 Henry VI*

1592–93	*Richard III*
1592–94	*Titus Andronicus*
1593–94	*The Taming of the Shrew*
1593–95	*The Two Gentlemen of Verona*
1594–96	*Romeo and Juliet*
1595	*Richard II*
1594–96	*A Midsummer Night's Dream*
1596–97	*King John*
1596–97	*The Merchant of Venice*
1597	*1 Henry IV*
1597–98	*2 Henry IV*
1598–1600	*Much Ado About Nothing*
1598–99	*Henry V*
1599	*Julius Caesar*
1599–1600	*As You Like It*
1599–1600	*Twelfth Night*
1600–01	*Hamlet*
1597–1601	*The Merry Wives of Windsor*
1601–02	*Troilus and Cressida*
1602–04	*All's Well That Ends Well*
1603–04	*Othello*
1604	*Measure for Measure*
1605–06	*King Lear*
1605–06	*Macbeth*
1606–07	*Antony and Cleopatra*
1605–08	*Timon of Athens*
1607–09	*Coriolanus*
1608–09	*Pericles*
1609–10	*Cymbeline*
1610–11	*The Winter's Tale*
1611–12	*The Tempest*
1612–13	*Henry VIII*

Poems

| 1592 | *Venus and Adonis* |
| 1593–94 | *The Rape of Lucrece* |

The Critics

The Play

When I saw this piece played in Drury Lane there stood behind me in the box a British beauty who, at the end of the fourth Act, wept passionately, and many times cried out, 'The poor man is wronged!' It was a countenance of noblest Grecian cut, and the eyes were large and black. I have never been able to forget them, those great black eyes which wept for Shylock!

When I think of those tears I must include *The Merchant of Venice* among the tragedies, although the fame of the work is a composition of laughing masks and sunny faces, satyr forms and amorets, as though the poet meant to make a comedy. Shakespeare perhaps intended originally to please the mob, to represent a thorough going wehr-wolf, a hated fabulous being who yearns for blood, and pays for it with a daughter and with ducats, and is over and above laughed to scorn. But the genius of the poet, the spirit of the wide worlds which ruled in him, was ever stronger than in his own will, and so it came to pass that Shylock, despite the glaring grotesqueness, expressed the justification of an unfortunate sect which was oppressed by providence. . . .

> —Heinrich Heine, 1839; quoted in Wilders, *A Selection of Critical Essays*

The Merchant of Venice is not a realistic drama; and its characters simply cannot be judged by realistic standards. Jessica, taken out of the context of the play, and exposed to the cold light of moral analysis, may be a wicked little thing; but in the play, wherein alone she has her being, she is nothing of the kind—she is charming.

. . . *The Merchant of Venice* is not a problem play;
it is a fairy story, within the framework of which
Shakespeare allowed free working to the thoughts
of his mind and the feelings of his heart.
—J. Middleton Murry in
Shakespeare, 1936

The Merchant of Venice is, among other things, as
much a problem play as one by Ibsen or Shaw. The
question of the immorality or morality of usury was
a sixteenth century issue on which both the theologians and the secular authorities were divided. . . .
—W. H. Auden, "Love and Usury
in *The Merchant of Venice*," 1965

On Harmony

Gratiano's excessiveness in the way of mirth and
laughter makes him the direct antithesis of Shylock,
who is notably deficient in these departments. And
when, at the trial, Gratiano capers about, taunting
Shylock and exulting in his discomfiture, this excessiveness (which in certain circumstances can be
attractive enough) is revealed in its more repulsive
aspect.
—Lawrence Danson, *The
Harmonies of The Merchant of
Venice*, 1978

Shylock

Is it by accident or design that Shakespeare allows
the Duke, as representative of Elizabethan propri-
ety, to philosophize about Christian mercy ("Thou
shalt see the difference of our spirits") minutes before he sanctions Shylock's unmerciful destruction?
Why was Portia, the playgirl of the Elizabethan
World, given that line of ultimate hypocrisy—"The
quality of mercy is not strain'd / It droppeth as the
gentle rain from heaven"—as a prelude to utterly
wiping out Shylock? Could Shakespeare have put
in Shylock's mouth that classic assault against dis-

crimination, "Hath not a Jew eyes . . ." if he wanted merely to create a hateful stereotype?

—Fred M. Hechinger, "Why
Shylock Should Not Be
Censored," *The New York Times*,
March 31, 1974

But the speech that to-day moves us is 'Hath not a Jew eyes?' etc. This is the speech not so much of a comic character as of a villain; and like other villains in Shakespeare he is given his due—a full chance to speak up for himself—while he holds the floor. But it seems quite impossible to take it as pathetic, so hedged about is it with prejudice, beginning on a note of thwarted avarice and of revengefulness, and ending on one of rivalry in revenge, of beating the Christians at what, however justly, he chooses to think of as their own game.

—E. E. Stoll, *Shakespeare Studies*,
1927

Shakespeare set out to write a comedy about a stage Jew involved in a grotesque story about a pound of flesh. But Shylock, to satisfy his author, must seem to act as a recognisably human being would behave in the given circumstances and Shakespeare has *humanised* him to such good purpose that this comic Jew has become, for many brilliant and sensitive critics, a moving, almost tragic, figure. Some even go so far as to exclaim of Shylock in his anguish: O what a noble mind is here o'erthrown!

. . . Shylock, since his motives must be more humanly comprehensible, is presented as a natural product of Christian intolerance, but he does not thereby cease to be a comic character or become an advocate of the humaner virtues.

—John Palmer, 1946; excerpted in
Wilders, *A Selection of Critical
Essays*

Antonio

. . . As Shylock is to Venetian society, so is Antonio to the world of love and marriage. The relationship of these two to these two worlds is the same, the relationship of an outsider. The play is, in effect, a twin study in loneliness. The fact that these two outcasts, these two lonely men, only meet in the cruel circumstances they do, adds an irony and pathos to the play which lift it out of the category of fairy tale romance.

—Graham Midgley, 1960; quoted in Tillyard, *Shakespeare's Early Comedies*